GOD

SECRETS

a life filled with

words of knowledge

WORKBOOK

TABLE OF CONTENTS

FOREWORD

Every generation seems to have individuals with unusual gifts and graces from God that cause people to stand in awe of Him. This generation is no different. The author Shawn Bolz and a small handful of others operate in such a spectacular anointing that I find myself overwhelmed with an awareness of the love of God for all of us. And while the gift he carries is rare, the ability and passion to train others to do the same is almost obsolete. Until now. Shawn Bolz is a profound communicator and displayer of the supernatural in such a way that it soon becomes our natural. If you have any desire or even a curiosity to bring an authentic supernatural lifestyle to the world around you, you will want *God's Secrets: Word of Knowledge Workbook*. It is absolutely priceless.

Bill Johnson
Bethel Church, Redding, CA
Author of *When Heaven Invades Earth and God Is Good*
BJM.org

INTRODUCTION

I t's time for all of us to grow in this amazing spiritual gift! Words of knowledge was given to us by God as a relational tool to help us know His innermost thoughts and that those thoughts can actually transform the world around you!

Inside this workbook, we've laid out the basic theology of words of knowledge. Each chapter provides teaching to help inspire and create faith in you, reflection questions, and personal and group activities. We've even included a chapter quiz to help you really understand this gift and the difference between it and the other revelatory gifts. Finally, we offer a prayer to help you identify and acknowledge where you are in the process of growing in words of knowledge, as well as to ask for this gift in greater measure.

I believe you're about to have a *huge* activation through this workbook, which will bring you the theology and practical steps of practice as well as the philosophy that will give you courage to experiment and risk! Whether you're on your own or in a group or class going through this workbook, I pray that you would not only have a download of faith for this amazing gift, but that you would also take leaps toward activating it into your life!

Shawn Bolz

FOUNDATION

"Now to each one the manifestation of the Spirit is given for the common good. To one there is given through the Spirit the message [word] of wisdom, to another the message [word] of knowledge by means of the same Spirit, to another faith by the same Spirit, to another gifts of healing by that one Spirit, to another miraculous powers, to another prophecy, to another the ability to distinguish between spirits, to another the ability to speak in different kinds of tongues, and to still another the interpretation of tongues. All these are the work of one and the same Spirit, and He gives them to each man, just as He determines."

1 Corinthians 12:7

CHAPTER OVERVIEW

- ○ 🕇 Invitation Scripture
- ○ ᧙ Getting to Know Words of Knowledge
- ○ 🖊 Four Teaching Points
- ○ 📋 Questions / Journal
- ○ ☑ Quiz
- ○ ☼ Individual Activities
  - ○ ⏱ Right Now Risk
  - ○ ▯ Lifestyle Opportunity
- ○ ⚭ Group Activities
- ○ 💬 Discussions
- ○ ✋ Prayer
- ○ 💬 Testimony

TEACHING POINTS

1. Biblical Basis for Words of Knowledge

2. Why Words of Knowledge
   Their Biblical Promise

3. Benefits
   An Invitation to Desire Words

4. How to Receive Words of Knowledge - *Desire, Zeal, Commissioning, Impartation*

Throughout Scripture, words of knowledge are rooted and grounded in the Word of God in so many ways. In each chapter of this workbook, we'll explore new biblical examples of how God has used this beautiful gift throughout history. I want to encourage you to take your time going through this workbook. Enjoy the first chapter on biblical foundations. Use the Chapter Overview to check off the sections you've completed. You'll find that each chapter and its Teaching Points coincide with the *God Secrets* book. My prayer is that this workbook will give you the practical counsel you need to apply the concepts in the book.

GETTING TO KNOW WORDS OF KNOWLEDGE

Instruction: Read and prayerfully consider the following Scripture references to words of knowledge. I pray you grow in your biblical understanding of how this gift has been used throughout God's Word.

1 IDENTIFYING PEOPLE BY NAME

Luke 19:5-6 When Jesus reached the spot, he looked up and said to him, "Zacchaeus, come down immediately. I must stay at your house today." So he came down at once and welcomed him gladly.

John 1:42 And he brought him to Jesus. Jesus looked at him and said, "You are Simon son of John. You will be called Cephas" (which, when translated, is Peter).

Acts 10:4-6 Cornelius stared at him in fear. "What is it, Lord?" he asked. The angel answered, "Your prayers and gifts to the poor have come up as a memorial offering before God. Now send men to Joppa to bring back a man named Simon who is called Peter. He is staying with Simon the tanner, whose house is by the sea."

2 IDENTIFYING JESUS IN SITUATIONS

Matthew 16:16-17 Simon Peter answered, "You are the Messiah, the Son of the living God." Jesus replied, "Blessed are you, Simon son of Jonah, for this was not revealed to you by flesh and blood, but by my Father in heaven.

Luke 2:36-38 There was also a prophet, Anna, the daughter of Penuel, of the tribe of Asher. She was very old; she had lived with her husband seven years after her marriage, and then was a widow until she was eighty-four. She never left the temple but worshiped night and day, fasting and praying. Coming up to them at that very moment, she gave thanks to God and spoke about the child to all who were looking forward to the redemption of Jerusalem.

3 IDENTIFYING INTIMATE PAST CHILDHOOD DETAILS

John 21:18 Very truly I tell you, when you were younger you dressed yourself and went where you wanted; but when you are old you will stretch out your hands, and someone else will dress you and lead you where you do not want to go."

4 KNOWING THE EMOTIONAL WELL-BEING OF SOMEONE

2 Kings 4:27 When she reached the man of God at the mountain, she took hold of his feet. Gehazi came over to push her away, but the man of God said, "Leave her alone! She is in bitter distress, but the Lord has hidden it from me and has not told me why."

CHAPTER ONE

TEACHING POINTS

NOTES

1 Biblical Basis for Words of Knowledge

The Bible is full of words of knowledge stories. In the Old Testament, we see prophets, leaders, and judges participating with this gift; and in the New Testament, we find a variety of examples, starting with Elizabeth who immediately knew Mary was pregnant with the Messiah. I love how Elizabeth's word of knowledge came when her own baby kicked within her. Only God could have revealed this kind of secret.

The examples go on: Ananias had a word of knowledge about Saul and went to commission him. He knew who and where Saul was, even down to the street name. Elisha got a clear picture of his servant Gehazi's lie in 2 Kings 5. In the New Testament, we read about Jesus seeing Nathaniel under the fig tree (see John 1:47-50), as well as Jesus knowing that the disciples were arguing about who was the greatest (see Mark 9:33-35). The apostles also had various stories of words of knowledge, and a study of early Christianity reveals that this spiritual gift garnered tremendous respect even after biblical times.

Because Scripture is filled with stories of words of knowledge, we have numerous examples that clearly show us various prototypes of this gift. Words of knowledge happened a lot and for many different reasons.

Their frequency and diverse purposes reveal a God who loves to share His thoughts and intentions with us about current and past events. The purposes are many: helping locate people; offering provision; identifying people; giving details about someone's life and death; showing who to appoint into leadership; revealing who would die and who was in the womb, etc. God has consistently throughout the Bible given divine knowledge to man so that we can fully relate to His goodness and eternal glory.

NOTES

God also uses words of knowledge to show that He is very present and very connected to us. He created this awesome gift to illuminate His heart and thoughts for us. He's God, so He could have chosen any number of ways to get the job done. But on numerous occasions, we see Him using people to share divine knowledge.

2 Why Words of Knowledge – Their Biblical Promise

In very real and real-time ways, words of knowledge help us connect to God's heart—not just the principles but the person of God.

Colossians 2:3 tells us, "In Christ are hidden all the treasures of wisdom and knowledge." Words of knowledge help us to treasure who Jesus is and apply this nature to our everyday lives. In the moment, they offer a revelation of the knowledge that is in Christ.

The Greek word for "wisdom" here is *sophia*, which is the knowledge of how to regulate one's relationship with God. It is a wisdom that is related to goodness. The word also describes someone who is spiritually prudent with others and knows how to access the Spirit to regulate circumstances: skillful, expert, sensible, judicious. It is the same word that Paul uses in 1 Corinthians 12:8 for "word of wisdom": "For to one is given the word of wisdom through the Spirit, and to another the word of knowledge according to the same Spirit."

In the Colossians verse, the word "knowledge" here is *gnosis*, which in this context means "to know experientially." It is present and fragmentary knowledge compared to the related word *epignosis*, which the Greeks used to convey a clear and exact knowledge gained through education or participation. *Gnosis* is an intuitive knowledge that is in the present. Again, it is the same word Paul uses in 1 Corinthians 12:8 to refer to a prophetic word of knowledge.

To know someone in a biblical sense was to have deep intimacy with that person. In fact, the Greek word for "know" or "knowledge" (*ginosko*) is the same one used in the context of sexual intimacy. Receiving and sharing words of knowledge isn't about gaining information. Studying the Greek shows us that this gift is about having intimate knowledge of the mind of God.

Our God is a just God, and words of knowledge in Scripture help us to see what He's doing now in our culture today. In the life of Daniel, we see one of the clearest pictures of social transformation and God's extraordinary protection over His people. God downloaded both spiritual knowledge and natural knowledge into the minds and hearts of Daniel and his friends (see Daniel 1:17). That special download helped the exiled Hebrew advise the Babylonian king and his kingdom. Daniel even interpreted King Nebuchadnezzar's dreams through words of knowledge, securing the whole course of Daniel's life and the destiny of his people.

If you could download the knowledge inside someone else's head into your own, how much would their perspective, life experience, and understanding affect yours? As we seek to know what God is thinking and what He cares about, we can literally get a transfusion of God's mind and heart in an everyday way through words of knowledge.

3   Benefits – An Invitation to Desire Words

When we walk in words of knowledge, we are not limited to our thoughts, opinions, education or socioeconomic status to relate to the world around us. We get God's thoughts—His expressed opinions—and we start to discover the substance of His eternal nature and promise here on Earth now.

All of us want solutions, an easier route to take that avoids the pitfalls and landmines of life. We all want the best advice for our relationships and the understanding to learn the most from our past experiences, good and bad. Words of knowledge provide both.

When you grow in intimacy with someone, you want to know how he or she thinks. You desire to know what makes him or her tick. You want to understand him or her. God gives us Scripture as the ultimate encounter with His nature, but He also couples His

NOTES

NOTES

Word with a relationship to His very Spirit. The Holy Spirit is a very real person who relates to us what the Father is thinking or saying, and what He intends for His creation.

As we start to understand the purposes of words of knowledge and what they can do, we begin to get hungry for this expression of the prophetic because it is such a relational connector to God. Words of knowledge help us to relate to people and situations in ways unique to experiencing this type of revelation. The unrelatable becomes relatable.

In his first letter to the church of Corinth, Paul shares that unless we speak in revelatory words of knowledge, prophecy or by some inspired doctrine (see 1 Corinthians 14:6), we won't profit someone in spiritual gifts. Then in verse 25, Paul shows us that these types of revelation reveal the secrets of a person's heart, causing us to know God through life-changing connection with Him.

I love the word "secrets" coupled with the word "heart" in verse 25. It is the word kruptos, describing both the concealed and private things of a person's life (secrets) and the innermost thoughts or feelings/emotions (heart).

In Acts 17:22-23, we see how God shared the secrets of his heart with Paul, as He gave Paul revelation to powerfully present the gospel to the people of Athens in a way that helped them really connect to it:

> So Paul took his stand in the open space at the Areopagus and laid it out for them. "It is plain to see that you Athenians take your religion seriously. When I arrived here the other day, I was fascinated with all the shrines I came across. And then I found one inscribed, to the god nobody knows. I'm here to introduce you to this God so you can worship intelligently, know who you're dealing with."

How amazing that God, whose glory fills the whole earth, desires to help His creation to see Him in all of life, causing humanity to know Him! Hunger for the revelation is not a gift alone, but a way to know His nature.

4 How to Receive Words of Knowledge—Desire, Zeal, Commissioning, Impartation

Spiritual gifts are different from natural gifts or talents in that the gifts of the Spirit are accessible to, and can be learned by, any of us. We all have God's Spirit in us who makes God's gifts available to us. This means that we can desire to grow in words of knowledge, pursue it, and excel in it. Paul tells us that God has given the different spiritual gifts to the body for the purpose of building up people. At the same time, in 1 Corinthians 14:1, he tells *everyone* to pursue the spiritual gifts. If God commands us to pursue something—so that we know we're aligned with His will—we won't fail at it.

Let's put it this way: Jesus says in Matthew 7:9-12, "Which of you, if your son asks for bread, will give him a stone? Or if he asks for a fish, will give him a snake? If you, then, though you are evil, know how to give good gifts to your children, how much more will your Father in heaven give good gifts to those who ask him! So in everything, do to others what you would have them do to you, for this sums up the Law and the Prophets."

Your heavenly father will only invite you into a gift that He's willing to give to you generously and beautifully. In John 16, Jesus says that the coming of the Holy Spirit would connect us to the Father. Then Paul describes the Holy Spirit as searching deep within the Father and within us, distributing the Father's thoughts to us. That is amazing!

There are some obvious tools in how to grow in these gifts, but below I list three that I think will be most helpful to you:

The power of story: Read the examples of biblical words of knowledge in Scripture and then listen or watch for prophetic models of words of knowledge in your life. Find some credible people who are modeling this gift and, in your hunger for it, ask God to help you grow from their story and example.

Commissioning: Whatever people group you're called to reach comes with the resource of spiritual gifts

NOTES

that God will invest in you and through you. As you grow in your spiritual calling and destiny, you can access more and more of His gifts to help you impact the world around you. God commissions or releases His authority on us so that we can access and grow in His gifts. When people are commissioned by God, He sends them with His authority to establish His kingdom throughout the world in specific ways.

Impartation: Of course, impartation is hugely important. In 2 Timothy 1, Paul tells Timothy to "fan into flame" the impartation that he received from the laying on of hands. There are definitely times to ask people who move in spiritual gifts to lay hands on you to impart by faith this spiritual gift.

NOTES

_____

_____

_____

_____

_____

QUESTIONS FOR JOURNALING

1. How do words of knowledge benefit those that give them and those that receive them?

_____

_____

_____

_____

2. What are some of the purposes of words of knowledge?

_____

_____

_____

_____

3. What are some ways you can build a solid foundation in your life to receive and give words of knowledge?

_____

_____

_____

_____

 QUIZ

Instruction: Have you ever wondered what the difference is between a word of knowledge, word of wisdom, word of discernment, and prophecy? I encourage you to read the scriptures below, identify the gift the verse reflects, and circle the correct answer.

A contextual understanding of these gifts is available // *on page 127 - 128*

Answer key available // *on page 141*

1. Acts 9:12 (NASB)

"And he has seen in a vision a man named Ananias come in and lay his hands on him, so that he might regain his sight."

    a. WORD OF KNOWLEDGE   b. PROPHECY

    c. DISCERNMENT   d. WORD OF WISDOM

2. Daniel 9:25 (NASB)

"So you are to know and discern that from the issuing of a decree to restore and rebuild Jerusalem until Messiah the Prince there will be seven weeks and sixty-two weeks; it will be built again, with plaza and moat, even in times of distress."

    a. WORD OF KNOWLEDGE   b. PROPHECY

    c. DISCERNMENT   c. WORD OF WISDOM

3. John 4:19 (NASB)

"The woman said to Him, 'Sir, I perceive that You are a prophet.'"

    a. WORD OF KNOWLEDGE   b. PROPHECY

    c. DISCERNMENT   d. WORD OF WISDOM

4. Luke 19:30-31 (NASB)

"Go into the village ahead of you; there, as you enter, you will find a colt tied on which no one yet has ever sat; untie it and bring it here. If anyone asks you, 'Why are you untying it?' you shall say, 'The Lord has need of it.'"

a. WORD OF KNOWLEDGE   b. PROPHECY

c. DISCERNMENT   d. WORD OF WISDOM

5. Matthew 22:15-22 (NASB)

"Then the Pharisees went and plotted together how they might trap Him in what He said. And they sent their disciples to Him, along with the Herodians, saying, 'Teacher, we know that You are truthful and teach the way of God in truth, and defer to no one; for You are not partial to any. Tell us then, what do You think? Is it lawful to give a poll-tax to Caesar, or not?' But Jesus perceived their malice, and said, 'Why are you testing Me, you hypocrites? Show Me the coin used for the poll-tax.' And they brought Him a denarius. And He said to them, 'Whose likeness and inscription is this?' They said to Him, 'Caesar's.' Then He said to them, 'Then render to Caesar the things that are Caesar's; and to God the things that are God's.' And hearing this, they were amazed, and leaving Him, they went away."

a. WORD OF KNOWLEDGE   b. PROPHECY

c. DISCERNMENT   d. WORD OF WISDOM

INDIVIDUAL ACTIVITIES

RIGHT NOW RISK

It's time to take your first risk. Ask God to highlight someone you haven't talked to in a long time. Now pray for them and ask God how they are doing (their basic mood in life). Now text them or call them with a life encouragement based on how you feel. See how they respond. Was your encouragement just nice to hear or was it was much needed? Either response is a success. Example: My person is Uncle Jim. I feel as though he is frustrated financially but I don't really know that. I text him: "Hey Uncle Jim, I just wanted to say hi and that I thought of you when I was reflecting on life today—just how much I appreciate your example of a good provider as a husband and dad. You are a great example!! Love ya, Shawn." Then he texts back, "Wow! Thanks! You have no idea how much that means to me right now!" or, "Good to hear from you." Either way is a win and gets you primed to pump your spiritual encouragement muscles.

LIFESTYLE OPPORTUNITY

Talk to five people you aren't that close to and purpose to get to know them. As you engage in conversation with each one, ask God how He feels about them. This exercise will develop your ear to hear God in the middle of everyday life while also building rapport with people with whom you might one day have the opportunity to share God's thoughts and love.

After your conversation, reflect on what you heard. Could you hear God clearly? How did what He revealed to you affect your conversation and how you saw the other person?

 GROUP ACTIVITIES

Share with your group what you've learned in both Scripture and daily life about words of knowledge. What would you like to experience further in this area? Share the most powerful word of knowledge you've ever witnessed even if it didn't come from you. Can you see yourself taking that kind of risk?

Once everyone has shared, pray as a group for the Lord to commission you in this gift. If anyone in the group already walks in words of knowledge, pray for impartation of this gift for the group.

 # DISCUSSIONS

Pick out one or two of your favorite word of knowledge scriptures. Why are they your favorite and what makes you identify with them? Share your thoughts with a friend or discuss in a group!

_____

_____

_____

_____

_____

_____

_____

_____

_____

_____

_____

_____

_____

_____

_____

_____

_____

_____

_____

 # PRAYER

Lord, thank You for helping me see the importance and purpose of words of knowledge. Continue to open my eyes to this gift within the Scriptures. I desire the gift of words of knowledge in my life and commit to continue to learn about this gift and how to operate in it. I ask that as I go through this workbook and resource, You would journey alongside me. I dedicate myself to learning, getting out of my comfort zone, and taking great risk. Lord, please bless my efforts to learn and form in me a great foundation for words of knowledge. I know You will increase my faith as I step out in loving people through the revelatory gifts. *In Jesus' Name. Amen.*

WORD OF KNOWLEDGE TESTIMONY

Keri Gardner

was at a conference where Shawn Bolz was speaking. Shawn had written down "Keri" and "Gardener." He asked if the words meant anything to anyone. I raised my hand and said, "My name is Keri Gardner." Then he asked if I have a "senior" and a "junior" in my family. I told him that my son is named after his grandfather and that we call him Robbie. Immediately, Shawn told me, "This word isn't about you; it's about your son."

Shawn said, "I feel like God wants to give you excitement on a new level for your role in life because you've sacrificed a lot to be a mom. You could have had a really intense career because you are a driven performer; you have an amazing work ethic. The Lord has shown me Robbie's life—that this young man is a champion leader of leaders who God is going to equip and train. Your son already has a heart for justice; he's always there for the underdog. He already cares about people that the world doesn't care about. I can already see it on him. There are so many examples, such as how he is with kids with disabilities.

"I feel like the Lord is showing you some of the things inside Robbie's heart that will make him great in his lifetime. I feel like the Lord wants to give you so much encouragement to help you understand that what you're doing right now to raise him will have so much significance, because when he comes into his own, he's going to help bring you into something. I don't know what that means, but I just saw him coming into his own, and I saw his purpose and you're not riding on his coattails or living vicariously through him. It wasn't like that. You literally had positional authority because of what he was doing. I don't know what that looks like or what that means, but I know he's a leader of leaders and the Lord loves him. There is a generational blessing that the grandfather and his father never fully entered into yet. Robbie is going to walk out the fullness of the dream of the family. They paid a price for it, but he gets to walk out the fullness of it.

"I feel like you are going to be so encouraged, like the Lord is saying, 'You're doing a great job,' and that He's so proud of you. He's so proud of your mothering. He's just so proud.

"Keri, you're doing it totally different than how you were raised. You're completely night-and-day different. Not that you were raised badly, but it's like you've learned from the strengths and weaknesses from how you were raised and the Lord is so proud of you for loving so well. Robbie feels so loved by you. I can tell. I feel like the

Lord is saying you're going to help speak into parenting in a wider way than you could have ever imagined because of what He's doing through you. People are going to want to know how you did this: 'How did you guys parent him because this is pretty amazing?' And I just want to encourage you that God is with you in a big way, Keri. Your family is your garden right now. And it's going to bear the biggest fruit you could ever imagine. Better than if you'd gone after your career at this point in your life. In the long-term, this garden will produce so much fruit that you'll feel like one of the richest people on Earth."

We received this word more than three years ago. We have yet to see total fulfillment of if, but we have seen God move. Robbie, at the time of the word, was suffering with ADHD and severe neck and back issues. Now, at 8 years old, his health is thriving, and he's focused on growing up to be the leader that Mr. Shawn said he was called to be.

INTIMACY

"Pursue love, yet desire earnestly spiritual gifts."

1 Corinthians 14:1

CHAPTER OVERVIEW

- ⊕ Invitation Scripture
- Getting to Know Words of Knowledge
- ⚒ Two Teaching Points
- Questions / Journal
- ☑ Quiz
- Individual Activities
  - ⏱ Right Now Risk
  - Lifestyle Opportunity
- Group Activities
- Discussions
- Prayer
- Testimony

TEACHING POINTS

1 Words of knowledge bring revelation that always prioritizes Jesus.

2 Your personal prayer life is the key to unlocking more words of knowledge. It is the only thing that will give you long-term fruit in pursuing revelation.

GETTING TO KNOW WORDS OF KNOWLEDGE

Instruction: Read and prayerfully consider the following Scripture references to words of knowledge. I pray you grow in your biblical understanding of how this gift has been used throughout God's Word.

1 APPOINTING POSITION

1 Samuel 16:3-5: "Invite Jesse to the sacrifice, and I will show you what to do. You are to anoint for me the one I indicate." Samuel did what the Lord said. When he arrived at Bethlehem, the elders of the town trembled when they met him. They asked, "Do you come in peace?" Samuel replied, "Yes, in peace; I have come to sacrifice to the Lord. Consecrate yourselves and come to the sacrifice with me." Then he consecrated Jesse and his sons and invited them to the sacrifice.

Acts 13:2: While they were worshiping the Lord and fasting, the Holy Spirit said, "Set apart for me Barnabas and Saul for the work to which I have called them."

2 IDENTIFYING PROVISION

Mark 14:12-16: On the first day of the Festival of Unleavened Bread, when it was customary to sacrifice the Passover lamb, Jesus' disciples asked him, "Where do you want us to go and make preparations for you to eat the Passover?" So he sent two of his disciples, telling them, "Go into the city, and a man carrying a jar of water will meet you. Follow him. Say to the owner of the house he enters, 'The Teacher asks: Where is my guest room, where I may eat the Passover with my disciples?' He will show you a large room upstairs, furnished and ready. Make preparations for us there." The disciples left, went into the city and found things just as Jesus had told them. So they prepared the Passover.

3 INTERPRETING DREAMS

Daniel 2:18-19: He urged them to plead for mercy from the God of heaven concerning this mystery, so that he and his friends might not be executed with the rest of the wise men of Babylon. During the night the mystery was revealed to Daniel in a vision. Then Daniel praised the God of heaven.

Genesis 40:8-12: Then Joseph said to them, "Do not interpretations belong to God? Tell me your dreams." So the chief cupbearer told Joseph his dream. He said to him, "In my dream I saw a vine in front of me, and on the vine were three branches. As soon as it budded, it blossomed, and its clusters ripened into grapes. Pharaoh's cup was in my hand, and I took the grapes, squeezed them into Pharaoh's cup and put the cup in his hand." "This is what it means," Joseph said to him.

4 KNOWING PERSONAL CHARACTER

John 1:47: When Jesus saw Nathanael approaching, he said of him, "Here truly is an Israelite in whom there is no deceit."

CHAPTER TWO

TEACHING POINTS

NOTES

1 **Words of knowledge bring revelation that always prioritizes Jesus.**

All revelation always has a source and focal point. While there is the subject and object of the revelation, behind it is the source of the connection: the Spirit of Jesus. Everything that God shows us is for the benefit of building up His Son's name in the world around us, or to help establish His dominion, love, strength, and even transformation so that He can one day inherit His great reward.

Like us, Jesus has a destiny. He paid a price on the cross to reconnect us to His Father. Until He returns, our whole life's goal and pursuit is to honor Him over pursuing our destiny or purpose. Because we are indebted to Jesus for what He did on the cross to restore us to His Father, we sacrifice personal gain as a primary goal. Any revelation we get shouldn't center on our working to build our life or world, but rather on building His life and power in others. Any influence and power we might gain is for the purpose of serving Him, knowing that when He paid that price on the cross, He also made us co-heirs who would rule and reign with Him when He returns.

This is important perspective for pursuing the revelation gifts. We should always prioritize Jesus as our focus. If this is the desire of your heart, you'll always have the right priority and connection to Jesus when you prophesy. When you can't find Jesus in the center of the gift, that's when you know that you are using discernment to build your own agenda.

Scripture reveals God's relational matter. It's a beautiful thing! He created us out of a deep desire to share His nature and build relationship. God isn't about just creating a system of leadership; He wants to create and raise up an eternal life partner, a best friend, even a bride (see Revelation 19).

NOTES

_____
_____
_____
_____
_____
_____
_____
_____
_____
_____
_____
_____
_____
_____
_____
_____
_____
_____
_____

As we draw closer to Jesus, His Spirit will come alive in us, translating the Bible for life application and good theology but also relating His thoughts for our daily life. He can't help but speak His mysteries and inner thoughts, downloading them to those He loves. He is not an independent God; the Trinity itself proves that. He thrives off connection, and it is His joy to share with us. He wants to be known.

As we grow in closeness to God and His thoughts, the revelation gifts impart to us His very nature. We start to get filled with knowledge and wisdom for our generation. This knowledge and wisdom are spiritual gifts for interpreting His secrets—with the potential to affect science, psychology, business, politics, education, environmental issues, civil rights issues, and more. It isn't limited to building just the Church.

Just picture one of those areas: kingship. When God imparted His knowledge and wisdom to King Solomon, people from every nation came just to hear him deliberate justice and rule his kingdom. It was so awesome that it became a spectacle. Solomon's supernatural knowledge affected the way he built his kingdom and influenced how justice reigned on a political and judicial scale, impacting not only Israel but also every known nation. He asked for this gift, and as a result, we see words of wisdom and words of knowledge downloaded into his very nature: "Give therefore thy servant an understanding heart to judge the people that I may discern between good and bad; for who is able to judge this so great a people?" (1 Kings 3:9).

The understanding that Solomon asks for is the Hebrew word *shama*, which means "to hear intelligently." Solomon asked that he would have God's intelligence to interpret whatever he heard. The word "discern" in Hebrew is *biyn*, meaning "to distinguish, be cunning, have intelligence or knowledge between; to understand."

Both words represent Solomon's request for wisdom—the first time in recorded history that a human solicited God for the power to think like He thinks. Solomon asked to have the mind of God, or knowledge and wisdom like His.

Through the life of Daniel and his friends, we can see the picture of revelation downloaded for the sake of education. Daniel 1:17 says, "As for these four youths God gave them knowledge and skill in all learning and wisdom and Daniel an understanding in all kinds of visions and dreams" (AMP).

The word "knowledge" used here is translated from *madda* in Hebrew. This is both the word for divine intelligence and also divine consciousness. It is a perfect description for words of knowledge where you have a divine consciousness of God's mind. This reflects both word of wisdom and word of knowledge, which brought them beyond a natural education and affected how their leadership impacted Babylon.

God longs to share the best of Himself with a people who would be trustworthy of His best. Words of knowledge assimilate us with His nature. Our mind is absorbed into His.

2   Your personal prayer life is the key to unlocking more words of knowledge. It is the only thing that will give you long-term fruit in pursuing revelation.

I've been around so many people who were hungry for the prophetic gifts but, even after God used them in wonderful ways, they lost their faith or walk with Him after just a few years. I have even seen incredibly gifted people with a season of life in the prophetic ministry not walk in their Christian faith five or ten years later. I think power gifts can give you a false sense of closeness to God. If your goals aren't centered on Him, prophetic gifts can give you a false sense of closeness. If you practice it only as a gift and not as a relational tool, you're at risk for feeling used by God or others. Or you'll only feel celebrated when you're operating in your gift or ministry, and you won't know how to relate to the world. In this light, you have the appearance of being God's best friend, but you don't even know Him. This kind of pseudo-living can lead to depression, crisis of faith, and even to spiritual suicide.

NOTES

NOTES

The only people I know who are still going in it are those whose identity and relationship with God are paramount. They aren't just pursuing a gift. Instead, they don't just hear God to do stuff or to minister to others. They have an awesome friendship with Him.

Many people who have a natural propensity for the spiritual gifts are so excited about them that they can become driven by them and sacrifice their personal relationship and intimacy with God. It's like when a married couple has kids and becomes high-functioning roommates, never or rarely having relationship with each other. This kind of marriage just can't be sustained; it's just a shell of what it's supposed to be.

You were made for connection. One of my co-workers, Jeremy, gets words of knowledge that show him how to apply Scripture to explore theology, which is way past his education level. The gift also brings him new ways of thinking about scriptural concepts. Jeremy's a modern-day reformation theologian in the making. He has such a great time unraveling Scripture, getting downloads of revelation. But then this drives him to know God in so many deep ways. He isn't just doing it to become a great teacher; Jeremy's captured by his affection for God.

My friend Todd White has taken on so much of God's love nature that prophecy seems organic to his very life. Whether he's with friends, family, or strangers, everywhere he goes the atmosphere fills with faith. When you're around him, you know that through Todd you're going to meet with God. In this intimacy with God, he just has raw faith. So it always feels like Todd is introducing you to his most passionate friend versus giving you a prophetic word or a word of knowledge.

Out of all the revelation gifts, words of knowledge can either make you feel extremely affectionate about the world around you or it can be used to puff up your ego and create a sense of arrogance. The other day, I was watching a TV minister who literally looked like he had built a following based on the authority of his accuracy in his words of knowledge versus the authority of his connection to people through the love of Jesus. If he keeps going this way, this minister will spend his whole ministry seeking more knowledge that keeps his platform puffed up versus resting in the fact that God is love. God's beautiful, unconditional love is the builder of the highest platforms.

These subtle differences in pursuit of the goals of intimacy and developing a gift around it versus developing a spiritual gift for any other goal will make or break your pursuit.

NOTES

QUESTIONS FOR JOURNALING

1. How do you feel your level of intimacy with the Lord affects the world around you?

_____

_____

_____

_____

_____

_____

2. Have you ever seen someone give a word of knowledge who didn't prioritize Jesus? What was the result?

_____

_____

_____

_____

_____

_____

_____

3. Has your relationship with the Lord grown as you have pursued the gift of words of knowledge?

_____

_____

_____

_____

_____

_____

4. How have you seen your prayer life affect your ability to receive and share words of knowledge?

_____

_____

_____

_____

_____

_____

 QUIZ

Instruction: Have you ever wondered what the difference is between a word of knowledge, word of wisdom, word of discernment, and prophecy? I encourage you to read the scriptures below, identify the gift the verse reflects, and circle the correct answer.

A contextual understanding of these gifts is available // *on page 127 - 128*
Answer key available // *on page 141*

1. Genesis 15:5 (NASB)

"And He took him outside and said, 'Now look toward the heavens, and count the stars, if you are able to count them.' And He said to him, 'So shall your descendants be.'"

a. WORD OF KNOWLEDGE   b. PROPHECY

c. DISCERNMENT   d. WORD OF WISDOM

2. 2 Kings 4:9 (NASB)

"She said to her husband, 'Behold now, I perceive that this is a holy man of God passing by us continually.'"

a. WORD OF KNOWLEDGE   b. PROPHECY

c. DISCERNMENT   c. WORD OF WISDOM

3. Mark 14:13-15 (NASB)

"And He sent two of His disciples and said to them, 'Go into the city, and a man will meet you carrying a pitcher of water; follow him; and wherever he enters, say to the owner of the house, "The Teacher says, 'Where is My guest room in which I may eat the Passover with My disciples?'" And he himself will show you a large upper room furnished and ready; prepare for us there.'"

a. WORD OF KNOWLEDGE   b. PROPHECY

c. DISCERNMENT   d. WORD OF WISDOM

4. Luke 4:1-14 (NASB)

"Jesus, full of the Holy Spirit, returned from the Jordan and was led around by the Spirit in the wilderness for forty days, being tempted by the devil. And He ate nothing during those days, and when they had ended, He became hungry. And the devil said to Him, 'If You are the Son of God, tell this stone to become bread.' And Jesus answered him, 'It is written, "Man shall not live on bread alone."' And he led Him up and showed Him all the kingdoms of the world in a moment of time. And the devil said to Him, 'I will give You all this domain and its glory; for it has been handed over to me, and I give it to whomever I wish. Therefore, if You worship before me, it shall all be Yours.' Jesus answered him, 'It is written, "You shall worship the Lord your God and serve Him only."' And he led Him to Jerusalem and had Him stand on the pinnacle of the temple, and said to Him, 'If You are the Son of God, throw Yourself down from here; for it is written, "He will command His angels concerning You to guard You," and, "On their hands they will bear You up, So that You will not strike Your foot against a stone."' And Jesus answered and said to him, 'It is said, "You shall not put the Lord your God to the test."' When the devil had finished every temptation, he left Him until an opportune time. And Jesus returned to Galilee in the power of the Spirit, and news about Him spread through all the surrounding district."

a. WORD OF KNOWLEDGE   b. PROPHECY

c. DISCERNMENT   d. WORD OF WISDOM

5. Matthew 16:16-18 (NASB)

"Simon Peter answered, 'You are the Christ, the Son of the living God.' And Jesus said to him, 'Blessed are you, Simon Barjona, because flesh and blood did not reveal this to you, but My Father who is in heaven. I also say to you that you are Peter, and upon this rock I will build My church; and the gates of Hades will not overpower it.'"

a. WORD OF KNOWLEDGE   b. PROPHECY

c. DISCERNMENT   d. WORD OF WISDOM

INDIVIDUAL ACTIVITIES

RIGHT NOW RISK

Stop and take a moment with the Lord. Ask Him to highlight a specific person in your life and ask Him to share with you His thoughts toward them. Imagine the God of all the universe dreaming of this person before the beginning of time. What were His dreams for him or her? What does He love about them? What inspires His heart about them?

The goal of this exercise isn't to get a word necessarily but to let God reveal how to honor and value someone you're praying about as you're gaining intimacy with Him.

Did you hear Him? What do you feel that He said? How did this exercise affect you?

LIFESTYLE OPPORTUNITY

I encourage you to schedule other times into your week to spend pursuing God. Spend time with Him cultivating intimacy, the fruits of the spirit, and gifts. Ask Him this week about the five core people in your life. Use the same questions in the RISK NOW section to know God's heart for them.

 GROUP ACTIVITIES

Partner with someone and pray for each other. Ask the Lord about your partner and listen for the secrets He shares. Try to listen for three to four different things and get ready to ask questions instead of being direct. Share with your partner what the Lord has said. This does not have to be a word of knowledge. It can be words that edify, encourage, and comfort. This will build a bridge to sharing words of knowledge as you begin to hear the Lord in new ways.

What kinds of words did you give? Words of knowledge, words of prophecy, discernment, words of wisdom? Identify them with your partner.

 # DISCUSSIONS

How do you set the goal of intimacy in pursuing words of knowledge?

_____
_____
_____

Remember a bad example of prophetic ministry that you've seen. Without naming anyone, what was the reason it had a negative impact on you? If you could go back and hijack the prophetic word, what do you think the focus should have been? How would you have changed the encounter?

_____
_____
_____
_____
_____

In what areas would words of knowledge be helpful in your life right now?

_____
_____
_____

For Group Activity: Did anyone get a word of knowledge? Share those stories. Ask the person who was the recipient how it made him or her feel?

_____
_____
_____
_____

 # PRAYER

Lord, as I pursue words of knowledge, help me to stay focused on You, or if necessary, to return to You, my first love. My desire is for deep, intimate relationship and connection with You. May everything I do be birthed out of love. I ask that You help me establish good life habits that will produce good fruit. I want to be a safe place where You can share You to develop our relationship. I ask for Your favor and blessing on this time and on our relationship. Come close as I pursue You. Teach me how to love well. I love You. *In Jesus' Name. Amen.*

WORD OF KNOWLEDGE TESTIMONY

Jared Stump

I heard the feet of one of my housemates pounding the floor above me.

"Jared!" he yelled. "Shawn is on the phone for you!"

I was a bit puzzled, as my phone was in my room, and I didn't know who this Shawn was. When I reached the top of the stairs, Brendan handed me his phone.

"Hello?" I asked, a bit apprehensively.

"Hey! Is this Jared?"

"Yes," I replied.

"Are you 22?"

"Yes ..." I replied again.

"Are your parents' names Randy and Alana?"

Yes again.

"Are they in Texas?"

Yes.

"Oh, okay," Shawn replied casually, before beginning to prophesy over them. This accurate word revealed things no one from the outside could have possibly known about my family. At one point, Shawn even referenced that God was removing negative things in our family line and "cutting them down to a stump."

Our last name is Stump.

Shawn then began to prophesy over me personally, calling out my writing gift and confirming several things God had already spoken to me privately. Unknown to him, I had written a book three years before but was intentionally keeping it on the down low until God said the moment was right. Within the year, I published *Creation & Redemption: Finding Your Place in a Fallen World*, the book I had written three years prior, and then embarked on a coast-to-coast book tour.

It's been two years since Shawn prophesied over my family, and I'm currently working on more books and operating a small business that helps authors and churches communicate more effectively.

3

DIRECTIVES OF
WORDS OF KNOWLEDGE

"For the Lord gives wisdom; From His mouth come knowledge and understanding."

Proverbs 2:6 (NASB)

CHAPTER OVERVIEW

- ⊹ Invitation Scripture
- ⊹ Getting to Know Words of Knowledge
- ✗ Four Teaching Points
- ▤ Questions / Journal
- ☑ Quiz
- ☼ Individual Activities
  - ⏱ Right Now Risk
  - ❙ Lifestyle Opportunity
- ⦾ Group Activities
- ▤ Discussions
- ✋ Prayer
- 💬 Testimony

TEACHING POINTS

1. God gives personal words of knowledge to you.

2. He shares words of knowledge for healing.

3. God gives words of knowledge for the world around us.

4. Words of knowledge bring justice/transformation.

GETTING TO KNOW WORDS OF KNOWLEDGE

Instruction: Read and prayerfully consider the following Scripture references to words of knowledge. I pray you grow in your biblical understanding of how this gift has been used throughout God's Word.

1   IDENTIFYING PAST ACTIVITIES AND SURROUNDINGS

John 1:48:   "How do you know me?" Nathanael asked. Jesus answered, "I saw you while you were still under the fig tree before Philip called you."

2   REVEALING PROPER IDENTITY/HIDDEN MOTIVES

1 Kings 14:5-6: But the Lord had told Ahijah, "Jeroboam's wife is coming to ask you about her son, for he is ill, and you are to give her such and such an answer. When she arrives, she will pretend to be someone else."

3   BUILDING PLANS (BLUEPRINTS FOR BUILDING)

Genesis 6:14-22: So make yourself an ark of cypress wood; make rooms in it and coat it with pitch inside and out. This is how you are to build it: The ark is to be three hundred cubits long, fifty cubits wide and thirty cubits high. Make a roof for it, leaving below the roof an opening one-cubit high all around. Put a door in the side of the ark and make lower, middle and upper decks. I am going to bring floodwaters on the earth to destroy all life under the heavens, every creature that has the breath of life in it. Everything on earth will perish. But I will establish my covenant with you, and you will enter the ark—you and your sons and your wife and your sons' wives with you. You are to bring into the ark two of all living creatures, male and female, to keep them alive with you. Two of every kind of bird, of every kind of animal and of every kind of creature that moves along the ground will come to you to be kept alive. You are to take every kind of food that is to be eaten and store it away as food for you and for them." Noah did everything just as God commanded him.

Exodus 35:30-35: Then Moses said to the Israelites, "See, the Lord has chosen Bezalel son of Uri, the son of Hur, of the tribe of Judah, and he has filled him with the Spirit of God, with wisdom, with understanding, with knowledge and with all kinds of skills—to make artistic designs for work in gold, silver and bronze, to cut and set stones, to work in wood and to engage in all kinds of artistic crafts. And he has given both him and Oholiab son of Ahisamak, of the tribe of Dan, the ability to teach others. He has filled them with skill to do all kinds of work as engravers, designers, embroiderers in blue, purple and scarlet yarn and fine linen, and weavers—all of them skilled workers and designers.

4 IDENTIFYING PREGNANCY AND PURPOSE

Matthew 1:20-21: But after he had considered this, an angel of the Lord appeared to him in a dream and said, "Joseph son

Getting to Know Words of Knowledge (Continued)

of David, do not be afraid to take Mary home as your wife, because what is conceived in her is from the Holy Spirit. She will give birth to a son, and you are to give him the name Jesus, because he will save his people from their sins."

Luke 1:11-17: Then an angel of the Lord appeared to him, standing at the right side of the altar of incense. When Zechariah saw him, he was startled and was gripped with fear. But the angel said to him: "Do not be afraid, Zechariah; your prayer has been heard. Your wife Elizabeth will bear you a son, and you are to call him John. He will be a joy and delight to you, and many will rejoice because of his birth, for he will be great in the sight of the Lord. He is never to take wine or other fermented drink, and he will be filled with the Holy Spirit even before he is born. He will bring back many of the people of Israel to the Lord their God. And he will go on before the Lord, in the spirit and power of Elijah, to turn the hearts of the parents to their children and the disobedient to the wisdom of the righteous—to make ready a people prepared for the Lord."

CHAPTER THREE
TEACHING POINTS

1 God gives personal words of knowledge to you.

God wants to speak to and through you—and not just for the benefit of everyone else. When we speak to someone, we share our nature with that person by giving of ourselves. We open a flow of relational connection. The prophetic gifts reinforce this exchange. I love how the New Testament Gospels provide examples of how Jesus tried to connect very personally to individuals based on the Father's love for them. Sometimes we get so caught up in trying to be like our model—none other than Jesus—that we look to receive His words and interpret Scripture so that we can effectively reach others. But it really starts with us.

NOTES

NOTES

God wants to speak to you about your life and help bring context to what He's doing in you. If you can interpret God for yourself, hearing Him speak about your circumstances, then you can easily give to others out of that overflow of His heart. So many people get this backward. They think they can't hear God for themselves. In fact, Gordon Lindsey (who used to document healing evangelists from the 1950s) made several statements saying how difficult it was for prophets and healers to hear God for themselves. They could hear Him for others but often found Him silent when it came to their own lives. I think this was the case because there was no model of relationship and personal connection to God for the sake of inward thriving.

It takes a lot of vulnerability to hear God for yourself, to know what He's saying about your present and past. But repeatedly I've seen (both in my life and in others) that when God does share His heart and mind with us about our own story, it is one of the most beautiful ways Christians can experience great growth. He has messages about who we are. I think of Peter in Acts 10:9-10 when he was caught up in a place of worship that became a heightened state of spiritual awareness with God called "trance":

> On the next day, as they were on their way and approaching the city, Peter went up on the housetop about the sixth hour to pray. But he became hungry and was desiring to eat; but while they were making preparations, he fell into a trance.

The Greek word for "trance" is *ekstasis*, which represents an ecstasy, also described as amazement and glory. Peter knew how to connect to God beyond the mental or emotional in ways that filled his mind and emotions with so much wonder. In this place, he got a word of knowledge through a vision. God showed him that he was supposed to go and minister to a people group outside the Jewish people. Of course this was a major change of direction, theology, and paradigm. Until then, he had only ministered and shared Jesus' gospel with his own Jewish people. But his heart was filled with love for the Gentiles. Even in the midst of this, however, he started to doubt what he had seen. Enter Cornelius. God gave him an encounter with an angel who shared with Cornelius a word of knowledge to "go and find Peter, the tanner." He even showed Cornelius where to find Peter! This is radical and beautiful. God changed Peter's paradigm not just for his ministry but also because He wanted to make Peter's life so much richer and fill it with greater purpose.

We're called to hear from God in very specific ways for ourselves. Because Jesus lives in your heart and mind, you are your own best personal prophet. He'll confirm what He has said to you and through you. But so many times, it will start *with* you, even through personal words of knowledge.

2   He shares words of knowledge for healing.

One of the most visible ways words of knowledge operate is in physical healing of the body. So many healing ministries have helped to model, demonstrate, and teach this great aspect of the word of knowledge gift. I love how John G. Lake, the famous healing evangelist from Spokane, Washington, would describe people's medical conditions in great detail, diagnose even what the doctors couldn't (though many times they were present in the meetings), and then pray for healing. Everyone was downright astonished when the person for whom he prayed was completely and miraculously healed.

Throughout the Gospels, Jesus operated in clear words of knowledge for healing. My favorite story is the woman with the issue of blood. He felt healing go out from Him and then shouted, "Who touched me?" Why? Because He knew someone had been healed. The woman was afraid to respond. Her medical condition had made her unclean. She knew she shouldn't have touched Him, but she was desperate enough to take the risk. Instead of the expected rebuke, she received unexpected blessing: "Your faith has healed you!" This story is one of dozens in which Jesus gets words of knowledge either directly about the condition of someone's health or, as we see in this example, a word of knowledge leads to the healing.

Words of knowledge for healing are an amazing as-

NOTES

NOTES

pect of the gift because they give us insight into the condition, compassion and empathy for the suffering person, as well as faith for the healing process or even an instantaneous miracle. I remember getting a word of knowledge over a lady in Rock, Colorado, about her stomach condition. I called her out by name and then described the condition as "stomach seizures"—exactly what the doctors were calling it. She was spontaneously healed of an illness that had no cure. It was such an isolated diagnosis that the fact I could name it when I (and no one else there) had never heard of it was a spectacle in itself that raised her faith level to receive the healing.

Words of knowledge open up the Spirit and body to receive the faith to align with God's will and plan. They create substance in someone's hope that allows for a radical and sometimes immediate change—even if it requires a miracle.

3 God gives words of knowledge for the world around us.

Of course, God wants to give us words to share with people in our lives, as well as with people we don't know. Sometimes meeting someone will come through a word of knowledge in which God shows us something about that person that compels us to talk to him or her. God gives us these so that someone can come into the knowledge of who Jesus is and connect with Him.

God may have you minister to individuals or over companies, nations, territories, people groups, industries, or even environmental issues. He cares about the world:

This is how much God loved the world: He gave his Son, his one and only Son. And this is why: so that no one need be destroyed; by believing in him, anyone can have a whole and lasting life. God didn't go to all the trouble of sending his Son merely to point an accusing finger, telling the world how bad it was. He came to help, to put the world right again. (John 3:16-17)

This is what words of knowledge do: they help someone feel rightly aligned with their Creator and Savior again.

I love the inner-healing prayer model that you may have heard about called *sozo*, the Greek word for fullness of salvation. The prayer is based on recalling memories or things you need to work through. You ask Jesus to reveal to you what He thinks about the memory or where He was in it. I've seen people even remember a painful childhood event they experienced before they were saved. Jesus shared clear pictures and words with them, showing them how strong His love and compassion is for them over this secret pain. *Sozo* is such a beautiful prayer model because it gives us the ability to apply good theology through an encounter in our lives. When this happens, we can get some real breakthrough prayer.

Words of knowledge do the same thing. They show us where Jesus is and was in different stages of our life and journey. They cause people to know God and enter into an awe for who He is to them personally.

4 Words of knowledge bring justice/transformation.

God's very nature makes Him a bringer of justice. God sent His Son to restore all things. Words of knowledge help us to see His intention, which can sometimes move things forward in radical ways. Whether it's a one-on-one issue in someone's life, such as a death, social injustice, racial discrimination, or any other injustice or exploitation, God can share His heart about that issue in ways that can forever change a person's life.

Let me give you an example of this in an unexpected encounter with a homeless man I ran into one day:

On a quick grocery store run, I went in expecting to get what I needed and be on my way. But as I walked through the aisles, everyone there seemed like a lost soul, like shells of people just going through the motions. As I walked past a woman who had clearly smoked a good part of her life, she gruffly growled, "Excuse me!" as if I had cut her off or done something to her. *Just get me out of here*, I thought. Before I

NOTES

NOTES

_____

_____

_____

_____

_____

_____

_____

_____

_____

_____

_____

_____

_____

_____

_____

_____

_____

_____

_____

_____

came in, I'd been listening to worship music in my car, and yet the atmosphere had not transitioned with me beyond the doors. As I hurried out, I saw him, the one that everyone looks past and ignores, a bum who I'm sure is used to his familiar spot. He only made initial eye contact with people coming in to see if they could give him anything.

It was a very hot day in Los Angeles, and I just wanted to get in my car, but this man was too alluring to the Spirit of love inside me. My attitude instantly adjusted. I went over to him and said, "I would like to do something for you. What can I do?"

He was nice at first. He wanted some water and food. I had some things in my grocery bags that he liked. Then he started a crazy conspiracy-focused, drug-addicted rant and almost turned on me.

"Whoa! Hold the conspiracy," I said. "I'm just a guy trying to value you."

I was smiling, but under my breath I was taking spiritual authority. He stopped and looked down—almost like someone had hit a reset button.

"I know who you are," he said. "God sends me good people to show me He still loves me. I don't let Him though, because of what I've done."

I was shocked. He was self-aware! God-aware! But because of shame, he was still rejecting the ultimate truth of God's love to touch his personal worthiness.

I quickly asked God, *What can I say to this hurting soul?* I didn't feel especially heroic or sense that this was one of those profound times to hear from God. But I put my hand on the back of his very smelly shirt and looked him in the eyes and said, "He will keep coming until you let Him in again. He just loves you too much. Do you remember the son in the prodigal son story? The father never looked at him as the wayward son. He just saw his son."

He had tears in his eyes. "Thanks for the food and the reminder," he said.

Then out of my mouth from the Spirit came the game changer. An insight or word of knowledge just popped out.

"Your son would forgive you if he was alive," I said. It was a very small but very transformational word of knowledge.

He looked at me, angry at first, and then started to cry. He cried for a while. I stood with my arm on his shoulder. Then he looked up at me. "Are you an angel?" he asked. "You have to be; that's how you knew."

I told him I wasn't but that I only knew because his son was in heaven with God, and God had told me about him.

He looked like he'd just had the weight of the world lifted off his shoulders, a million times lighter. I wrote down our church's name and told him to come by.

"If you're ready to pursue real life again, come find God. I'll help you," I told him. We prayed together, and I could tell he felt totally different.

"I might be ready," he whispered.

I hugged him and left him to ponder everything that had just happened. His desperation pushed me toward personal gratitude: *Man, I am so glad God is in me and that His love can compel me.*

My encounter with this man offers great evidence that through words of knowledge, we can affect root issues in society. This spiritual gift can bring resolution so much faster than counseling, therapy, rehabilitation, etc. Words of knowledge don't negate any of those things because many times people still need a process. But we need breakthrough first!

I was in South Korea, and a family who owns a large manufacturing company met with me for a very specific reason: They wanted confirmation on something God had showed them about their resource. We had dinner, and they took me to the manufacturing plant. We prayed together, and it was good. But I had no prophetic words for them. As we said

NOTES

NOTES

goodbye, they handed me a financial gift. "No, please give it to the poor that God has called your company to support," I said. "I have been in a season of giving 40 percent to the poor." They freaked out! That was the exact question they were looking for confirmation on—how much to give to the poor. They had started their multimillion-dollar company with a justice heart when they saw how poorly North Korean orphans in China were being treated. The couple had agreed to give exactly 40 percent, but their board members and family felt it was too much. Then here I come along, and through happenstance—not even knowing I was sharing a word of knowledge—showed them that God had blessed them with resources and wealth for a purpose, not just to prosper for their own benefit. Words of knowledge help define God's desire and intention toward the world.

QUESTIONS FOR JOURNALING

1. Do you feel that God has given you personal words of knowledge?

_____
_____
_____
_____
_____
_____
_____
_____

2. What types of words of knowledge have you experienced the most (words of healing, words for others, words for where to find your keys)?

_____
_____
_____
_____
_____
_____
_____
_____

3. At this stage in the workbook, how do you feel about taking risks to go after the gift of words of knowledge?

_____
_____
_____
_____
_____
_____
_____

 QUIZ

Instruction: Have you ever wondered what the difference is between a word of knowledge, word of wisdom, word of discernment, and prophecy? I encourage you to read the scriptures below, identify the gift the verse reflects, and circle the correct answer.

A contextual understanding of these gifts is available // *on page 127 - 128*
Answer key available // *on page 141*

1. Genesis: 45:5-8 (NASB)

"Now do not be grieved or angry with yourselves, because you sold me here, for God sent me before you to preserve life. For the famine *has been* in the land these two years, and there are still five years in which there will be neither plowing nor harvesting. God sent me before you to preserve for you a remnant in the earth, and to keep you alive by a great deliverance. Now, therefore, it was not you who sent me here, but God; and He has made me a father to Pharaoh and lord of all his household and ruler over all the land of Egypt."

a. WORD OF KNOWLEDGE   b. PROPHECY

c. DISCERNMENT   d. WORD OF WISDOM

2. 2 Kings 6:8-12 (NIV)

"Now the king of Aram was at war with Israel. After conferring with his officers, he said, 'I will set up my camp in such and such a place.' The man of God sent word to the king of Israel: 'Beware of passing that place, because the Arameans are going down there.' So the king of Israel checked on the place indicated by the man of God. Time and again Elisha warned the king, so that he was on his guard in such places. This enraged the king of Aram. He summoned his officers and demanded of them, 'Tell me! Which of us is on the side of the king of Israel?' 'None of us, my lord the king,' said one of his officers, 'but Elisha, the prophet who is in Israel, tells the king of Israel the very words you speak in your bedroom.'"

a. WORD OF KNOWLEDGE   b. PROPHECY

c. DISCERNMENT   c. WORD OF WISDOM

3. Mark 2:8 (NIV)

"Immediately Jesus knew in his spirit that this was what they were thinking in their hearts, and he said to them, 'Why are you thinking these things?'"

a. WORD OF KNOWLEDGE   b. PROPHECY

c. DISCERNMENT   d. WORD OF WISDOM

4. Deuteronomy 18:15 (NIV)

"The Lord your God will raise up for you a prophet like me from among you, from your fellow Israelites. You must listen to him."

a. WORD OF KNOWLEDGE   b. PROPHECY

c. DISCERNMENT   d. WORD OF WISDOM

5. 1 Samuel 9:15-21 (NIV)

"Now the day before Saul came, the Lord had revealed this to Samuel: 'About this time tomorrow I will send you a man from the land of Benjamin. Anoint him ruler over my people Israel; he will deliver them from the hand of the Philistines. I have looked on my people, for their cry has reached me.' When Samuel caught sight of Saul, the Lord said to him, 'This is the man I spoke to you about; he will govern my people.' Saul approached Samuel in the gateway and asked, 'Would you please tell me where the seer's house is?'

"I am the seer,' Samuel replied. 'Go up ahead of me to the high place, for today you are to eat with me, and in the morning I will send you on your way and will tell you all that is in your heart. As for the donkeys you lost three days ago, do not worry about them; they have been found. And to whom is all the desire of Israel turned, if not to you and your whole family line?'

"Saul answered, 'But am I not a Benjamite, from the smallest tribe of Israel, and is not my clan the least of all the clans of the tribe of Benjamin? Why do you say such a thing to me?'"

a. WORD OF KNOWLEDGE   b. PROPHECY

c. DISCERNMENT   d. WORD OF WISDOM

INDIVIDUAL ACTIVITIES

RIGHT NOW RISK

Ask the Lord for three personal words of knowledge, being intentional to ask Him for specific details for each word. Write down these words and the details in a journal or safe place. Date them. As the Lord continues to speak to you about each one, add these words to the ones you initially heard. As fulfillment of these words begins to happen, check back on your original words to see how clearly you hear the Lord speaking to you.

Pick one of the following categories—healing, the world around you, justice, or transformational word—and ask the Lord for a specific word of knowledge. If you receive a word of knowledge, ask Him what your next step is with that word. Then take action on what you hear.

LIFESTYLE OPPORTUNITY

For each day this week, ask God for words of knowledge either for yourself or for people you already know. Take a risk and share it. Write down the outcome.

 GROUP ACTIVITIES

Form a circle and have someone stand or sit in the middle of it. You're going to be a prayer team for someone this person in the circle knows very well and wants to see come to faith in Jesus. Begin as a group to ask God for words of knowledge that can help you pray for this friend, and then start asking the person in the middle questions: "Is this person older? Are they are woman? Do they work in the restaurant industry? Do they have a back problem?" Whenever you get any words right, ask God why He showed you them and then pray these words over this person. If the exercise produces certain words the person in the middle thinks their friend needs to know about, look for special ways to give them these words. I've seen people make a recording or write a letter, saying, "We had a prayer time for you as Christians, and this is what God showed us."

▦ DISCUSSIONS

Has God given you personal words of knowledge to help you in life? Share a story.

_____
_____
_____
_____

Have you ever seen or participated in a detailed word of knowledge for healing and the person received their miracle?

_____
_____
_____
_____
_____

Have you ever seen a word of knowledge that resolved or spoke God's heart toward a justice issue? How could a word of knowledge affect a justice issue impacting you or your family?

_____
_____
_____
_____
_____
_____
_____

 PRAYER

Lord, thank You for words of knowledge and the powerful effect they have. I first and foremost ask that You would help me begin to hear personal words of knowledge for myself. Tune my ears to hear You and my eyes to see You moving. Father, I want to be the best prophet to myself. I ask that You would help me explore each type of word of knowledge and provide me with opportunities for growth in each type. Bring full understanding and deep revelation of how You want to use words of knowledge through me. *In Jesus' Name. Amen.*

WORD OF KNOWLEDGE TESTIMONY

Heather Nunn

On this particular night, my husband and I were weary and, being the spiritual giants that we are, opted for Indian takeout and movies instead of going to the meeting where Shawn Bolz was speaking. At about 9:30 p.m., I began scrolling through Facebook when I noticed a friend who was at the meeting. She had just begun to Periscope the words of knowledge. I jumped onto Periscope and five minutes later, while staring at my iPhone, heard Shawn say, "This is a weird one, but I saw two things: a nun who lives on Olive Meadows Drive." My heart skipped a beat as I sat stunned, and then heard, "...possibly named Heather." He had just called out my name and the street we've lived on for eighteen years.

I quickly communicated with my Periscoping friend, and a few moments later saw Shawn's face staring back at me on my screen.

He said, "Heather, I felt like God said that He's going to anoint the worship gathering you're doing. It's a prototype and He's going to release a gathering anointing on you as a worship leader, but also as a leader to gather people and do something crazy like festivals and events that are going to change the worship culture of this region—Orange County and SD [San Diego] regions."

I was awestruck. The very next weekend, I was scheduled to host a regional conference for San Diego with my mentor Dan McCollam for a ministry I founded called One Sound. Our vision is to equip, empower, and encourage the creative worship voice of a region to see revival and transformation come to a city.

As if that weren't enough, God had more, and it was meant to touch my entire family. I started feeling compelled to tell Shawn about my brother. Just as the thought entered my mind, Shawn said to me, "God also said that *a seed went into the ground*" and gave June 29 as a birthdate of someone and that "what the seed went into the ground for is blossoming a prophetic worship movement, and that's going to mean something to you." At this point, I was *totally* undone. My younger and only brother, Peter Johnston, died tragically in a fall on June 2, 2014, at the age of 38. His birthday is June 29. He was a powerful and prophetic psalmist who had carried a worship movement in his heart for many years. When he died, my family picked up the mantle of his life to carry out what he had started.

We have begun to see this word Shawn gave me unfold in our lives. We just had our fourth annual One Sound conference last October, and I just launched a four-month worship mentorship program called AMP (Academy of Modern Psalmists), which is designed to equip and empower those who are called to transform culture through worship and the creative arts. Did I mention that my brother envisioned that name years ago? Yes, Lord, let it blossom indeed.

ACCOUNTABILITY

"For I long to see you, that I may impart to you some spiritual gift, so that you may be established."

Romans 1:11 (NKJV)

CHAPTER OVERVIEW

- ⊟ Invitation Scripture
- ⎗ Getting to Know Words of Knowledge
- ✗ Four Teaching Points
- ▤ Questions / Journal
- ☑ Quiz
- ☼ Individual Activities
  - ⏱ Right Now Risk
  - ▯ Lifestyle Opportunity
- ⬡ Group Activities
- ▤ Discussions
- ✍ Prayer
- 💬 Testimony

TEACHING POINTS

1. Tracking words/feedback gives you the opportunity to grow.

2. To grow in this gift, you need to create an internal rating system.

3. Recognize where to grow in character as you pursue prophetic gifts.

4. Core values are essential for pursuing words of knowledge.

GETTING TO KNOW WORDS OF KNOWLEDGE

Instruction: Read and prayerfully consider the following Scripture references to words of knowledge. I pray you grow in your biblical understanding of how this gift has been used throughout God's Word.

1 UNVEILING OF SIN IN SOMEONE'S LIFE

Joshua 7:10-11: The Lord said to Joshua, "Stand up! What are you doing down on your face? Israel has sinned; they have violated my covenant, which I commanded them to keep. They have taken some of the devoted things; they have stolen, they have lied, they have put them with their own possessions."

John 6:70-71: Then Jesus replied, "Have I not chosen you, the Twelve? Yet one of you is a devil!" (He meant Judas, the son of Simon Iscariot, who, though one of the Twelve, was later to betray him.)

2 DISCOVERING TRUTH / UNCOVERING A LIE

2 Kings 5:25-27: When he went in and stood before his master, Elisha asked him, "Where have you been, Gehazi?" "Your servant didn't go anywhere," Gehazi answered. But Elisha said to him, "Was not my spirit with you when the man got down from his chariot to meet you? Is this the time to take money or to accept clothes—or olive groves and vineyards, or flocks and herds, or male and female slaves? Naaman's leprosy will cling to you and to your descendants forever." Then Gehazi went from Elisha's presence, and his skin was leprous—it had become as white as snow.

3 FINDING PEOPLE / LOST PROPERTY

1 Samuel 9:19-20: "I am the seer," Samuel replied. "Go up ahead of me to the high place, for today you are to eat with me, and in the morning I will send you on your way and will tell you all that is in your heart. As for the donkeys you lost three days ago, do not worry about them; they have been found. And to whom is all the desire of Israel turned, if not to you and your whole family line?"

4 RECOVERING THE KIDNAPPED

1 Samuel 10:21-22: Then he brought the tribe of Benjamin near by its families, and the Matrite family was taken. And Saul the son of Kish was taken; but when they looked for him, he could not be found. Therefore, they inquired further of the Lord, "Has the man come here yet?" So the Lord said, "Behold, he is hiding himself by the baggage."

CHAPTER FOUR
TEACHING POINTS

1   Tracking words/feedback gives you the opportunity to grow.

While you're learning something, the best way to grow is to have a clear process with lots of feedback. For some reason in most of the church space, growing in the prophetic has always been left up to a mystical, personal journey. The reality is that God would never give us gifts to pursue that we couldn't excel in; and to excel in anything, it must be definable and quantifiable.

TWO TYPES OF FEEDBACK:

1. Getting Feedback While You're Sharing
There's nothing worse than someone who speaks a run-on sentence for God and states some inaccurate black-and-white facts and, because of their authoritative, almost arrogant, delivery style, allows absolutely no course correction. If you're sharing with someone and leave no room for feedback, they may not forgive your error in your risk taking. If I say, "God is going to heal Margaret, your mother!" and that person's mother was named Julie and is already dead, then I've lost them—but not necessarily because of my inaccuracy, but because of my arrogant tone that gives no leeway for correction.

Learning to get feedback as you go requires an interactive style that, admittedly, can be pretty uncomfortable and in some circles is actually even discouraged. I want to encourage you to ask questions and learn the difference between your thoughts and God's.

If you feel like the person you're sharing with has a dog, you're allowed to ask about it. Getting feedback can also open up a conversation that helps give you indicators pointing to what to ask God for or how to interact with someone. We've been taught that if we already have information about someone, we can't be useful. But the gifts of the Spirit all work

NOTES

_____
_____
_____
_____
_____
_____
_____
_____
_____
_____
_____
_____
_____
_____
_____
_____
_____
_____
_____
_____
_____
_____

best through the deep love we have for others. They are relational gifts, which means that the more we know about someone, the deeper we will pursue their spiritual breakthrough and advancement because we know that the word of knowledge and word of wisdom gifts are part of our prophetic tool set. And our prophetic gifts are also relational tools.

When you ask for feedback from the person to whom you're ministering, you discover that what you were feeling, sensing, or trying is right or wrong. That discovery has numerous benefits. The main one being that the more you begin to get someone's story right, the more you'll understand your process for getting and sharing words of knowledge. Another benefit is the fact that you will strive to course correct and maybe even evaluate differently the rest of the message you might want to deliver.

2. Feedback After the Encounter

When you're actually stepping out in faith and taking risks with words of knowledge and prophecy, it's important that you track your words in the future. In my previous book, *Translating God* (the spiritual successor to *God Secrets)*, I define some of the tracking process for prophecy. But for words of knowledge, you may not have the same future responsibility to an individual. The word might be fulfilled after the one encounter with the person. If the person with whom you're communicating is someone you can come back to later and ask for feedback, by all means do it. In the moment, the individual may be excited, touched, and overwhelmed. After he or she has had time to process the word you stewarded and walk it out a bit, getting feedback can be instrumental to your growth. Maybe the word was life changing; maybe it was just a great encouragement. Either way, to hear about its impact after the encounter would be good for you.

To get that feedback, you can just email or call and ask them. For example: "Hi, I'm in a growth process, learning how my personal ministry to others is helping them. Can I get feedback on the time I prayed with you or shared with you?"

This gives the individual the ability to process your request in a very straightforward way. If you get any negative feedback, that's okay because you'll learn from that as well. When you really want to learn, you'll want to hear any feedback (positive or negative), even if it's uncomfortable.

2 To grow in this gift, you need to create an internal rating system.

Developing your own internal weights and balance system is essential. How is your revelation coming to you? Is it strong, and can you bank on it? Or is it more of an unclear impression? Do you feel the presence of God when you get a revelation, or are you more cerebral? What is or isn't working for you personally? None of us is the same in how we relate to others, which means none of us will be the same in how we relate to God.

When I train people directly, I help them come up with their own internal rating system. This system isn't based just on feelings but on actual feedback and accuracy. In one large seminar (1,400-plus people), we asked a volunteer to stand up front. Then people began to share words of knowledge about this young man. I asked everyone to ask God for his name (on-demand assignments hardly ever work, but they can lead to some really touching moments). As people guessed every kind of name you could think, a woman raised her hand and asked, "Is this even possible? How will we ever know how to get a name?" That same person then said a name, and it was the volunteer's name!

Then I told the woman who had asked the question, "Now I want you to ask the Lord about someone in his life about whom he is most concerned and ask God for the name of that person."

She looked exasperated but tried anyway. She guessed a name, and it was wrong. Then another name that was wrong. Then she closed her eyes and prayed and tried again, and it was right! It was *exactly* who our volunteer was thinking about. We got a beautiful impartation of God's heart for this person and prayed for him.

NOTES

NOTES

_____

_____

_____

_____

_____

_____

_____

_____

_____

_____

_____

_____

_____

_____

_____

_____

_____

_____

_____

_____

When I asked the woman how she felt now, she said, "I could start to tell the difference when it was just a mental exercise and when I was tapping into God's mind."

This is exactly a clear picture of what happens when you ask for words of knowledge and practice getting them. It also helps you in the future when you don't have the same experience or confidence about something you've said. The word comes with a lighter weight, which means you can rate it differently and take an easier risk with it. For me, each type of information that seems like revelation comes with a sense of how heavy or light I feel about it. Do I feel level one (just a fleeting thought) or do I feel level ten (absolutely hearing from God)?

A rating system even helps you in communicating with friends and church members. You can say to them, "I feel really strongly about this." Or, "This is just a light impression, but I thought it might be helpful." Or even, "I believe I have heard from God." This can give you a sense of growing in areas, such as getting certain types of words of knowledge, that you have yet to develop. I have a pretty good idea when I'm getting a name, but so far I have a terrible time getting words of knowledge about politics (although I've gotten many prophecies about the future for different political people). I'm learning how to have an internal rating system, which helps me to take steps of faith in different ways.

Without an internal rating system, you might treat every type of revelation like it's extremely God, or extremely not God, and you won't assign the proper weight it needs to be delivered or received correctly.

3 Recognize where to grow in character as you pursue prophetic gifts.

"But what happens when we live God's way? He brings gifts into our lives, much the same way that fruit appears in an orchard—things like affection for others, exuberance about life, serenity. We develop a willingness to stick with things, a sense of compassion in the heart, and a conviction that a basic holiness permeates things and people. We find ourselves involved in loyal commitments, not needing to force our way in life, able to marshal and direct our energies wisely" (Galatians 5:22-23, THE MESSAGE).

Scripture is clear that if we're growing in our relationship with God, we will produce spiritual fruit. The stronger we grow in our walk, the more fruit we'll produce. There is a direct correlation. If you're trying things and don't have fruit after fifty or more tries, you need to change something. You might need a new process, a sphere you're trying to grow in, a delivery method, or even some personal development. In many circles, this can be discouraging because most churches don't measure the fruit of our growth in the prophetic gifts. Unless it's an essential word that moved the church forward, most churches don't celebrate it. You typically won't find a process of graduation from stage to stage like there is with other gifts, talents, and professions.

We can create an atmosphere of growth by doing the following: track words, share failures, celebrate successes.

Track words: When your words are right, celebrate them. Track with one or two friends who care about your spiritual journey in the prophetic (and hopefully are on their own) and tell them the story. For them, faith comes from hearing, and for you, faith gets solidified as you rehearse what God has done through you.

Share failures: When it feels like you've gotten thirty to fifty things correct (based on feedback), you can start to see that you've matured and have authority in that area. When you've gotten five hundred to one thousand correct, you can start to be a trusted advisor in that area. When it's one thousand to twenty thousand, you'll start to gain a reputation of credibility outside of your current environment.

Celebrate successes: Establish a trusted prophetic relationship to a local community such as a home group, a church, or ministry school. Sometimes people tell me, "My church doesn't offer prophetic ministry." That is true of a large majority of churches, but experience has shown me that in almost every region or even online, you can find a supportive community that will help you grow. In this community, you

NOTES

NOTES

can start to track words, share failures, and celebrate successes.

4   Core values are essential for pursuing words of knowledge.

In training many people in the prophetic, especially words of knowledge, we have to lay some ground rules that sound obvious but are so helpful when you begin your journey.

Core Value 1: Qualify what you already know. If you have any pre-knowledge of information that you're using to prophesy, always qualify that. Sometimes when I'm in front of people prophesying, I will say someone's name that I already I know. If I don't qualify that I already know this information, other people, even their family, might think that's part of the encounter or mistake it for revelation. If I know any information, I qualify everything when I'm sharing with more than one person in the room: "John, we know each other. I want to share something with you." So, everyone in the room knows I knew John's name. Or, "Sandy, I know you work in fashion. I just wanted to bring some revelation to that." That way people know what I know.

Core Value 2: Qualify if you've researched anything. Don't research or look up anything unless you tell people you did it. I have a young prodigy who does some research on people he's ministering to before he meets with them. He looks through the websites for their church, business or individual website or Facebook page (if they have them). It helps him get a heart to pray for them more specifically, *but* (and this is a big but) he tells them he has done that and doesn't allow himself to use any of the information on the website as if it's prophesy. If he found it there, he tells them it's there. I, however, hardly ever look at any websites or Google anyone I'm going to be with. Sometimes, I'll research them after the meeting if I discover they're a well-known individual, because that can be exciting. I'm old-fashioned and like to go in blind most of the time. Either way, the goal is to qualify what you know or have read so that you don't sound like you know more about them based on your revelation versus what you've read about them.

Core Value 3: Be honest about what you don't know. People pursuing revelation can come across as mystical and spiritual know-it-alls. Be honest about who you are and use vulnerability and your own weaknesses to relate to people. Don't always relate out of your strength. Seek God's strength. I love self-deprecation as long as it's not false humility. You don't want to appear more anointed than you actually are because you just can't maintain that. For years, people would try to put more exaggerated prophetic pressure on me by telling stories about me or comparing me to major prophetic voices of the past. That would cause others to want to relate to me in a more mature way than my gifting could take. My job was to have a right assessment of myself that wasn't too low or too high. With the right view, I don't allow appearance of an anointing that I can't operate in right now.

Core Value 4: If you're prone to exaggeration, lying or misinformation, catch yourself! Most of the prophetic people I know either underplay their words and personal prophetic stories or they overexaggerate them and sometimes claim things that just didn't happen. I remember asking a pastor friend why he didn't ever invite one of my favorite prophets to his church anymore and he told me a story.

"We were sharing a hotel room, and he woke up and told me he had a dream about Jesus and it was a good dream. I was supposed to leave that day but was able to stay for his session. He didn't know that I was still there and told the congregation, 'Last night, I had a face-to-face visitation with Jesus, and even my roommate saw Him with me!'"

It just wasn't true and the reality was that the prophetic person had upgraded his experience, either because he didn't have faith in how it came, or because he didn't have the confidence that it was enough. If that person can make that mistake, then many others can too.

There are many other core values for operating in the prophetic, but these will be helpful starters to develop as you pursue words of knowledge.

NOTES

QUESTIONS FOR JOURNALING

1. Are you used to getting feedback when getting words of knowledge? In what form does most of your feedback come?

_____

_____

_____

_____

_____

_____

2. Have you put any systems or processes in place to create personal accountability?

_____

_____

_____

_____

_____

_____

_____

3. What do you feel is your greatest area of opportunity for growth?

_____

_____

_____

_____

_____

_____

4. What makes feedback so impactful? How have you seen feedback produce growth in your life or someone else's? Apply feedback to the prophetic. Think of a prophecy that someone gave you in the past. If that person were here now, how could you give him or her feedback?

_____

_____

_____

_____

_____

_____

 QUIZ

Instruction: Have you ever wondered what the difference is between a word of knowledge, word of wisdom, word of discernment, and prophecy? I encourage you to read the scriptures below, identify the gift the verse reflects, and circle the correct answer.

A contextual understanding of these gifts is available // *on page 127 - 128*
Answer key available // *on page 141*

1. Matthew 17:27 (NIV)

"But so that we may not cause offense, go to the lake and throw out your line. Take the first fish you catch; open its mouth and you will find a four-drachma coin. Take it and give it to them for my tax and yours."

a. WORD OF KNOWLEDGE   b. PROPHECY

c. DISCERNMENT   d. WORD OF WISDOM

2. John 2:19-22 (NIV)

"They replied, 'It has taken forty-six years to build this temple, and you are going to raise it in three days?' But the temple he had spoken of was his body. After he was raised from the dead, his disciples recalled what he had said. Then they believed the scripture and the words that Jesus had spoken."

a. WORD OF KNOWLEDGE   b. PROPHECY

c. DISCERNMENT   c. WORD OF WISDOM

3. Acts 21:10-11 (NASB)

"As we were staying there for some days, a prophet named Agabus came down from Judea. And coming to us, he took Paul's belt and bound his own feet and hands, and said, 'This is what the Holy Spirit says: "In this way the Jews at Jerusalem will bind the man who owns this belt and deliver him into the hands of the Gentiles."'"

a. WORD OF KNOWLEDGE   b. PROPHECY

c. DISCERNMENT   d. WORD OF WISDOM

4. Micah 5:2 (NIV)

"But you, Bethlehem Ephrathah, though you are small among the clans of Judah, out of you will come for me one who will be ruler over Israel, whose origins are from of old, from ancient times."

a. WORD OF KNOWLEDGE   b. PROPHECY

c. DISCERNMENT   d. WORD OF WISDOM

5. Acts 23:6 (NASB)

"But perceiving that one group were Sadducees and the other Pharisees, Paul began crying out in the Council, 'Brethren, I am a Pharisee, a son of Pharisees; I am on trial for the hope and resurrection of the dead!'"

a. WORD OF KNOWLEDGE   b. PROPHECY

c. DISCERNMENT   d. WORD OF WISDOM

INDIVIDUAL ACTIVITIES

RIGHT NOW RISK

If you've given words of knowledge before, write down two words of knowledge that you've given someone. Now contact the person and ask the following questions:

How has this word impacted your life?
Do you feel the word was accurate?
Do you feel like you've had any fulfillment of this word?
How can I help steward this word I shared?

If you haven't shared words of knowledge with someone before, then think about a time you received a prophecy of any type. Describe the feedback you would have given the person if you had the chance. Then think about these questions:

How impactful was the word?
How accurate was the word? (Use percentages.)

Was there any fulfillment of the word? If not, do you still have hope for fulfillment?

How have you stewarded the word you received?

Did it help you connect to God more deeply or think about something differently?

▯ LIFESTYLE OPPORTUNITY

Each day this week, pick one of your Christian friends on social media (Facebook, Instagram, Twitter, etc.) whom you don't know well and write them a prayer. Try to use something that God showed you with words of knowledge. At the end of the letter, ask for feedback: "Does this make sense? Is this helpful?" Then send it with love.

 GROUP ACTIVITIES

Let's practice! Break up into pairs and give a word of knowledge to someone in the group. Ask for feedback. Whether or not the word was correct, be honest with the person about your internal rating system. How strongly did you feel the word was from God? How did the outcome / feedback affect your rating system?

DISCUSSIONS

Do you have an internal rating system for words of knowledge? What areas of this gift do you feel more confident in giving (healing words, time tables in people's lives, words about family, words about someone's business, words about ministry calling or gifts, etc).

In which of the core values we went through do you sense the greatest need for growth? What are some intentional steps you can take to grow in this area?

_____

_____

_____

_____

_____

_____

_____

_____

_____

_____

_____

_____

_____

_____

_____

_____

_____

PRAYER

Lord, I want to walk in words of knowledge with maturity. Grow me in this tool that reflects Your love so well. Help me to hear You with detail, clarity, and accuracy. As I begin receiving words of knowledge from You, give me the courage to stay accountable to what I share with others. I desire to walk in integrity with the gift of words of knowledge. I ask You to surround me with community that will support me as I develop this gift. I choose to create a system for myself to track my words. I commit to ask for feedback after I give a word. Thank You, Lord, for guiding me in my growth journey with words of knowledge. *In Jesus' Name. Amen.*

WORD OF KNOWLEDGE TESTIMONY

I remember walking through our local mall and seeing a woman from another country working hard to get her two toddlers and stroller up the escalator. It was obvious that the rude Americans trying to get by her were judging her for choosing to take the escalator instead of trying to find an elevator. The air was filled with tension as the people waited impatiently behind her, irritated over this small act of a mom trying to get to the next level of the mall. One man even pushed past her, completely ignoring her plight and knocking a bag out of her hand.

I ran over and grabbed the stroller and her bag while she managed the kids. By the time we got up the escalator, her frustration had almost turned to tears. I could tell this small incident probably played into some very real-life circumstances her family was going through. She thanked me over and over. I was about to walk away, but as I said goodbye to her cute little crew, I felt heaven pull on my heart to take a risk.

"Can I ask you something?" I said. "I'm having a spiritual moment and wanted to know if you're moving soon because of your husband's job?"

She looked shocked. "Yes!" she responded. Without questioning the spirituality of my moment or that I even had one, she opened her heart (which seems to be the common response when this happens) and told me their whole story. Her husband had been estranged from his family and family business, but his stepfather was dying, so his brother had reclaimed the business. He wanted to share it with his brother. They were moving to Texas to start a new life, but she was feeling so nervous about the move.

"Being from Ukraine, I have never been to Texas," she said with an amazing Eastern European accent.

"Is your husband's name Steve?" I asked. She said no.

At this point, I could have stopped there, let my insecurities take over, forgotten that this was not about me but about what God wanted to say to her, and ruined the moment. But I felt an inner prompting: *Stay engaged with her, Shawn; don't worry about you.*

So I went for broke.

"I'm a Christian, and I feel like God is showing me that He's restoring your husband's family and the family business to give your kids the legacy that is their birthright. This move to Texas is from Him!"

She had tears in her eyes. It seemed as if something inside her shifted and lifted the pressure and fear. She literally fell into me with a hug.

"You are not only going to be okay," I continued, "but God is moving in this and wants to help you in all of it. He is good."

She looked at me and replied, "I have never known God could speak or be like this."

Over the next twenty minutes, two miracles happened. I shared the gospel with her and she asked Jesus to show her who He was. The second was more subtle, but as a parent I knew God had intervened: Her toddler kids stayed completely absorbed with each other and were at peace, giving her the opportunity to ask questions and listen uninterrupted (any parent knows that's a true miracle). Later, I found out her husband already knew Jesus but hadn't really connected to his faith in decades. That changed as they moved back into their God-sent promised land.

DEVELOPING A LIFESTYLE OF RISK

"But earnestly desire the best gifts. And yet I show you a more excellent way."

1 Corinthians 12:31 (NKJV)

CHAPTER OVERVIEW

- ✝ Invitation Scripture
- 🔀 Getting to Know Words of Knowledge
- ✖ Four Teaching Points
- 📋 Questions / Journal
- ☑ Quiz
- ☼ Individual Activities
  - ◔ Right Now Risk
  - ▯ Lifestyle Opportunity
- ⧉ Group Activities
- 📄 Discussions
- 🖐 Prayer
- 💬 Testimony

TEACHING POINTS

1 Learn to be a risk-taker.

2 Performance issues will restrict opportunities to grow in words of knowledge.

3 Learn to identify and avoid the top three performance issues with words of knowledge.

4 Identity issues will take over who you are and God's purpose for your gifts.

GETTING TO KNOW WORDS OF KNOWLEDGE

Instruction: Read and prayerfully consider the following Scripture references to words of knowledge. I pray you grow in your biblical understanding of how this gift has been used throughout God's Word.

1   KNOWING THE HISTORICAL STATE OF THE CHURCH

Revelation 2–3

2   GETTING DIRECTIONS / ASSIGNMENT

Acts 9:11-12: The Lord told him, "Go to the house of Judas on Straight Street and ask for a man from Tarsus named Saul, for he is praying. In a vision he has seen a man named Ananias come and place his hands on him to restore his sight."

Acts 16:9-10: During the night Paul had a vision of a man of Macedonia standing and begging him, "Come over to Macedonia and help us." After Paul had seen the vision, we got ready at once to leave for Macedonia, concluding that God had called us to preach the gospel to them.

3   OFFERING WORDS FOR HEALING

Acts 9:17-19: Then Ananias went to the house and entered it. Placing his hands on Saul, he said, "Brother Saul, the Lord—Jesus, who appeared to you on the road as you were coming here—has sent me so that you may see again and be filled with the Holy Spirit." Immediately, something like scales fell from Saul's eyes, and he could see again. He got up and was baptized, and after taking some food, he regained his strength.

Acts 14:8-10: In Lystra there sat a man who was lame. He had been that way from birth and had never walked. He listened to Paul as he was speaking. Paul looked directly at him, saw that he had faith to be healed and called out, "Stand up on your feet!" At that, the man jumped up and began to walk.

4   RESURRECTION

John 11:4: When he heard this, Jesus said, "This sickness will not end in death. No, it is for God's glory so that God's Son may be glorified through it."

CHAPTER FIVE

TEACHING POINTS

NOTES

1 Learn to be a risk-taker.

Risk is the only way we'll grow in spiritual gifts. Unless they're practiced, they can't be perfected. When you strike a wrong note learning to play the piano, you only get the ringing of bad sound in your own ears. But making a mistake while learning something that requires God's nature often causes us to be overly cautious.

God is in charge of His own reputation and entrusts us with responsibility in this, but ultimately we can't destroy His image. It is everywhere. The whole earth is filled with Him. I have even met people who have come out of a deep spiritual abuse from cults, but eventually they could see the difference between God's goodness and the misuse of Christianity at the hands of some demented people.

I say this because so many of us are afraid of being wrong, afraid of making God look bad, afraid of the unknown, and afraid of persecution. On top of this, our society is littered with social anxiety, lack of self-awareness, and very little emotional intelligence. It's filled with performance issues.

When you start to learn to take risk though, you have to overcome your desire to be right and even the desire to make God look good. He is already perfect. You don't have to manufacture anything. You just have to be the best version of love you can be.

Risk is an awkward thing because it holds no guarantees. When Olympic athletes spend years training for an event, they don't know if they'll win, but the reality is that they're still world-renowned athletes. No one can take that away from them. We're already loved by God and in relationship with Him—this is enough! We get to risk with what He's showing us. I'll be the first to say that words of knowledge are one of the hardest gifts to risk with because they cre-

NOTES

ate a black-and white moment. You're either right or wrong. You're dealing with absolutes. The good thing is that getting something right should never be the goal of your encounter. Your goal should be love. Words of knowledge are just one of the relational tools you're using. If that tool doesn't work, you can still pull out another tool to love well.

During a recent trip to the barber, I thought I was getting a revelation for a man who was in line with me and asked him if he had a house in Laguna. He said, "No, why?" So I changed the subject, and we had a great conversation. He forgot that I had even asked him the initial question that I was hoping would turn into a radical prophetic encounter. He still felt valued, honored, and cared for as he walked away. Many times, we want to make the encounter more spiritual than it has to be. "I have a word for you!" doesn't have to lead our conversation. We can start with a little lower risk and still get an awesome result.

Risk is still risk though. When you're trying to share a word of knowledge that doesn't work out, the person will most likely question what you're trying to do and might even judge you for trying. The individual might feel that you're trying to do tricky evangelism. Avoid a bait-and-switch approach; no one appreciates it. Don't dangle something in front of someone to get their interest and then trick them into having a long conversation on something they don't want to hear about. All of society is wary of this approach. Our job is to be as authentic as possible and to honor someone's time.

When risk pays off, it's so empowering! When you have those wins in your faith, it gives you courage and builds up the muscle of faith.

2   Performance issues will restrict opportunities to grow in words of knowledge.

Performance issues will absolutely block you from growing in a healthy thriving prophetic gift. They will create lesser goals for you to try and master while the main goal of love and even enjoying God-given gifts goes to the wayside.

3 Learn to identify and avoid the top three performance issues with words of knowledge.

A. The desire to be right: This first performance issue kills people because it puts priority on the information itself instead of loving the person you're ministering to. At that point, because you're focused on the accuracy of the content, you're doing a job, not making a relational connection. This will cause the people to whom you share either to put up their defenses when you approach them or, if the encounter is somewhat successful to miss the God who's the source of the message, because you're focusing on the accuracy of the information, instead of the relationship. Knowledge can be healing, and I have made the mistake of highlighting the knowledge without helping people really understand where the knowledge is coming from and how it's connecting. Then it's more of a basic encouragement ("You have nice hair") than a spiritual connection ("God made your hair").

B. Focusing on delivery vs. focusing on the person: So many people try to get their presentation right. It's so important to become a good host of the Holy Spirit. But you can't focus more on your delivery of the word than on the people the word is for and who they are to God. They mean the world to Him. Sometimes, people who are prophesying don't stop to take in the masterpiece of God to whom they are about to speak and instead get caught up in the words or approach they're using. Authenticity and love are the greatest on-ramp to a vulnerable God connection with someone.

C. The desire to be awesome: Whether or not you want to look awesome or it's more subtle that that, this isn't the goal. The "awesome" factor comes into the play in the right area when you think about the true awe-worthiness of connecting to God the Creator in this way. Simply put, you just want to give people an awesome encounter with God. The reality is that a lot of things God does are quieter and more hidden than we might want them to be. He plants seeds that He'll water in other ways. I've seen people who get into prophetic evangelism in dangerous ways be-

NOTES

NOTES

cause they set the goal on the number of souls they will get saved versus the number of lives they get to love. Farmers can't just focus on harvesting. They have to be willing to till, plant, water, fertilize, weed, and *then* harvest. Prophetic encounters happen for many reasons, and we have to trust God, who is the Lord of the harvest field. We're just there to play a role in His love. I've missed out on some encounters with His love because my goals for power encounters were too overpowering. When you have to look amazing or powerful, or feel you have to make God look amazing or powerful, you'll sacrifice the person or people to whom you're ministering in order to hit this other goal.

4   Identity issues will take over who you are and God's purpose for your gifts.

When your identity becomes your gift, you're no longer existing. You are you; your gifts serve you—not the other way around. You don't serve your gifts. Prophetic gifts are tools to help God shine in and through you. They help you live a thriving life.

Just like we see some pop culture figures' personal lives implode because they sacrificed everything at the altar of their performance gift, many people who get involved in spiritual gifts tend to get caught up in the gift itself, or they get engulfed in the title or entitlement they get out of the gift. They only find joy or happiness when they perform the gift. On top of that, they stop being normal or stop contributing in all the other normal ways.

QUESTIONS FOR JOURNALING

1. What would risk taking in the area of words of knowledge look like for you?

_____
_____
_____
_____
_____
_____

2. When sharing a word of knowledge, do you feel like your personality or lack of emotional or social intelligence hinders you in any way? How can you overcome that? (Remember that most of these things you perceive as personal weakness are just areas you don't have tools for yet.)

_____
_____
_____
_____
_____
_____
_____
_____

3. Have you seen in your life or someone else's life that taking a risk to give words of knowledge brought great reward? Share about it.

_____
_____
_____
_____
_____
_____

4. Do you struggle with any of the performance issues we identified?

_____
_____
_____
_____
_____

 QUIZ

Instruction: Have you ever wondered what the difference is between a word of knowledge, word of wisdom, word of discernment, and prophecy? I encourage you to read the scriptures below, identify the gift the verse reflects, and circle the correct answer.

A contextual understanding of these gifts is available // *on page 127 - 128*
Answer key available // *on page 141*

1. Acts 8:23 (NLT)

"... for I can see that you are full of bitter jealousy and are held captive by sin."

        a. WORD OF KNOWLEDGE   b. PROPHECY

        c. DISCERNMENT   d. WORD OF WISDOM

2. Genesis 41:1-37 (NASB)

"Now it happened at the end of two full years that Pharaoh had a dream, and behold, he was standing by the Nile. And lo, from the Nile there came up seven cows, sleek and fat; and they grazed in the marsh grass. Then behold, seven other cows came up after them from the Nile, ugly and gaunt, and they stood by the other cows on the bank of the Nile. The ugly and gaunt cows ate up the seven sleek and fat cows. Then Pharaoh awoke. He fell asleep and dreamed a second time; and behold, seven ears of grain came up on a single stalk, plump and good. Then behold, seven ears, thin and scorched by the east wind, sprouted up after them. The thin ears swallowed up the seven plump and full ears. Then Pharaoh awoke, and behold, it was a dream. Now in the morning his spirit was troubled, so he sent and called for all the magicians of Egypt, and all its wise men. And Pharaoh told them his dreams, but there was no one who could interpret them to Pharaoh.

Then the chief cupbearer spoke to Pharaoh, saying, 'I would make mention today of my own offenses. Pharaoh was furious with his servants, and he put me in confinement in the house of the captain of the bodyguard, both me and the chief baker. We had a dream on the same night, he and I; each of us dreamed according to the interpretation of his own dream. Now a Hebrew youth was with us there, a servant of the captain of the bodyguard, and we related them to him, and he interpreted our dreams for us. To each one he interpreted according to his own dream. And just as he interpreted for us, so it happened; he restored me in my office, but he hanged him.'

Then Pharaoh sent and called for Joseph, and they hurriedly brought him out of the dungeon; and when he had shaved himself and changed his clothes, he came to Pharaoh. Pharaoh said to Joseph, 'I have had a dream, but no one can interpret it; and I have heard it said about you, that when you hear a dream you can interpret it.' Joseph then answered Pharaoh, saying, 'It is not in me; God will give Pharaoh a favorable answer.' So Pharaoh spoke to Joseph, 'In my dream, behold, I was standing on the bank of the Nile; and behold, seven cows, fat and sleek came up out of the Nile, and they grazed in the marsh grass. Lo, seven other cows came up after them, poor and very ugly and gaunt, such as I had never seen for ugliness in all the land of Egypt; and the lean and ugly cows ate up the first seven fat cows. Yet when they had devoured them, it could not be detected that they had devoured them, for they were just as ugly as before. Then I awoke. I saw also in my dream, and behold, seven ears, full and good, came up on a single stalk; and lo, seven ears, withered, thin, and scorched by the east wind, sprouted up after them; and the thin ears swallowed the seven good ears. Then I told it to the magicians, but there was no one who could explain it to me.'

Now Joseph said to Pharaoh, 'Pharaoh's dreams are one and the same; God has told to Pharaoh what He is about to do. The seven good cows are seven years; and the seven good ears are seven years; the dreams are one and the same. The seven lean and ugly cows that came up after them are seven years, and the seven thin ears scorched by the east wind will be seven years of famine. It is as I have spoken to Pharaoh: God has shown to Pharaoh what He is about to do. Behold, seven years of great abundance are coming in all the land of Egypt; and after them seven years of famine will come, and all the abundance will be forgotten in the land of Egypt, and the famine will ravage the land. So the abundance will be unknown in the land because of that subsequent famine; for it will be very severe. Now as for the repeating of the dream to Pharaoh twice, it means that the matter is determined by God, and God will quickly bring it about. Now let Pharaoh look for a man discerning and wise, and set him over the land of Egypt. Let Pharaoh take action to appoint overseers in charge of the land, and let him exact a fifth of the produce of the land of Egypt in the seven years of abundance. Then let them gather all the food of these good years that are coming, and store up the grain for food in the cities under Pharaoh's authority, and let them guard it. Let the food become as a reserve for the land for the seven years of famine which will occur in the land of Egypt, so that the land will not perish during the famine.' Now the proposal seemed good to Pharaoh and to all his servants."

a. WORD OF KNOWLEDGE   b. PROPHECY

c. DISCERNMENT   c. WORD OF WISDOM

3. 1 King 19:15-16 (NIV)

"Then the Lord told him, 'Go back the same way you came, and travel to the wilderness of Damascus. When you arrive there, anoint Hazael to be king of Aram. Then anoint Jehu grandson of Nimshi to be king of Israel, and anoint Elisha son of Shaphat from the town of Abel-meholah to replace you as my prophet.'"

a. WORD OF KNOWLEDGE   b. PROPHECY

c. DISCERNMENT   d. WORD OF WISDOM

4. John 1:43-51 (NASB)

"The next day He purposed to go into Galilee, and He found Philip. And Jesus said to him, 'Follow Me.' Now Philip was from Bethsaida, of the city of Andrew and Peter. Philip found Nathanael and said to him, 'We have found Him of whom Moses in the Law and also the Prophets wrote—Jesus of Nazareth, the son of Joseph.' Nathanael said to him, 'Can any good thing come out of Nazareth?' Philip said to him, 'Come and see.' Jesus saw Nathanael coming to Him, and said of him, 'Behold, an Israelite indeed, in whom there is no deceit!' Nathanael said to Him, 'How do You know me?' Jesus answered and said to him, 'Before Philip called you, when you were under the fig tree, I saw you.' Nathanael answered Him, 'Rabbi, You are the Son of God; You are the King of Israel.' Jesus answered and said to him, 'Because I said to you that I saw you under the fig tree, do you believe? You will see greater things than these.' And He said to him, 'Truly, truly, I say to you, you will see the heavens opened and the angels of God ascending and descending on the Son of Man.'"

a. WORD OF KNOWLEDGE   b. PROPHECY

c. DISCERNMENT   d. WORD OF WISDOM

5. Isaiah 7:14 (NASB)

"Therefore the Lord Himself will give you a sign: Behold, a virgin will be with child and bear a son, and she will call His name Immanuel."

a. WORD OF KNOWLEDGE   b. PROPHECY

c. DISCERNMENT   d. WORD OF WISDOM

INDIVIDUAL ACTIVITIES

RIGHT NOW RISK

After our focus on identity in the last chapter, I'm now going to challenge you to step out of your comfort zone. If you're an extrovert, challenge yourself to spend time with just the Lord, asking Him for words of knowledge about someone specific. Then ask Him how you are to deliver the word. If you're an introvert, take a risk and go out and talk to people. As you're talking to them, ask the Lord what He has to say to them and about them.

LIFESTYLE OPPORTUNITY

A challenge for everyone is to get out of their own bubble/comfort zone! Ask the Lord how you can partner with Him in giving words of knowledge to different people groups from different walks of life. Make sure to write down how this exercise affected you. What were people's reactions?

 # GROUP ACTIVITIES

Form groups of three to four people. Now that you're growing in theology and understanding for words of knowledge, let's do an assignment where we're only going after words of knowledge and putting all of the other revelation gifts on hold.

Pick one person in the group to think of someone. Make sure he/she doesn't share about the person in his/her thoughts. The other members should then take a moment to ask the Lord for words of knowledge about the person the other group member is thinking about. Start asking for specific words that identify what's precious to this person's life right now. Ask God to show you about this person's most important relationships, favorite food, or color, and then ask the Holy Spirit to show you details. You may not get any of these details, but you can use them as catalysts for how to ask questions. As you try out words of knowledge, don't second-guess yourselves. Are any of them accurate? Do this exercise several times, each time choosing a different person in the group to think of someone. This exercise will help you to recognize when you're hearing yourself versus when you're hearing the Lord.

Remember that this isn't a familiar process for most people and it may feel like a guessing game at first. You have to be patient with your own progress, and frustration can be a normal part of anyone's growth. In our culture, we want instant results. But words of knowledge are a relational skill with God, not just a gift. And any relationship takes time to develop.

 # DISCUSSIONS

What was the hardest part about the activation? What was the most enjoyable part?

Contrary to popular belief, we're all risk-takers in some way or another. In what areas in life are you a natural risk-taker? Maybe it's with moving to or vacationing in new places. Maybe it's with developing new relationships or with finances or investments. How can you apply that same risk-taking nature to your relationship with God when it comes to stepping out in the prophetic?

What is your favorite spiritual risk of any kind that has paid off? (Example: Mine is pursuing my wife and also following a risky decision to buy a property we felt God led us to purchase for our family.) Share about a risk and a little bit of the process. Share when you faced your fear.

_____
_____
_____
_____
_____
_____
_____
_____
_____
_____
_____
_____
_____
_____
_____

 # PRAYER

Lord, it's time to risk! I desire risk, as I know it brings results when developing the gift of words of knowledge. I ask for the grace and courage to take risk and do things in faith. I will look for opportunities that will take me out of my comfort zone. Raise my level of faith as I step out and attempt new things. Place me in the middle of divine appointments and unconventional meetings that lead to moments of risk. I pray that You bless these times and bring to life my faith and the faith of those around me when they see me sharing words of knowledge. I will risk! I will grow! *In Jesus' Name. Amen.*

WORD OF KNOWLEDGE TESTIMONY

About a year ago, I was at a meeting on the East Coast. Racial tension had been percolating across the country and in some places had come to a boiling point. I had been praying (still am) that God would bring spiritual resolution.

At the meeting, I asked a woman, "Is there a Daniel in your life? Was he violated by corrupt cops when he was a teenager and then two more times in his twenties when he was wrongfully arrested and even assaulted?"

It was her son.

"Go and tell him that this wasn't God and that it was a misuse of authority. This was an assignment from the enemy to rob Daniel of his authority because your son is a man of authority. He will hear this word from God and realize who God made him to be. He won't let anyone rob him again!"

She was crying. When she played for Daniel the word I had for him, the burden of these abusive situations he had been carrying around seemed to just melt away. Trauma released.

The fruit of this word was so awesome! A few weeks later, Daniel signed up for the police academy. Come on, God! It was his secret dream, and these traumatic experiences had robbed him of it. He couldn't change the past until God showed up and restored him.

I love this moment! It shows me that the prophetic gifts can be used to initiate resolution in some of the deepest issues in the world.

RECEIVING FROM GOD

"But the Helper, the Holy Spirit, whom the Father will send in my name, he will teach you all things and bring to your remembrance all that I have said to you."

John 14:26

CHAPTER OVERVIEW

- ○ 🕇 Invitation Scripture
- ○ 🔁 Getting to Know Words of Knowledge
- ○ ✖ Four Teaching Points
- ○ 📋 Questions / Journal
- ○ ☑ Quiz
- ○ ⚙ Individual Activities
  - ○ ⏱ Right Now Risk
  - ○ 📕 Lifestyle Opportunity
- ○ ⤙ Group Activities
- ○ 📰 Discussions
- ○ 🙌 Prayer
- ○ 💬 Testimony

TEACHING POINTS

1 God speaks to us in numerous and diverse ways.

2 Internal dialogue requires us to know when we're hearing our thoughts vs. hearing God's thoughts.

3 Pressing in for a greater measure of the gift requires intentionality and practice.

4 Setting a goal to be specific will help you grow in words of knowledge.

GETTING TO KNOW WORDS OF KNOWLEDGE

Instruction: Read and prayerfully consider the following Scripture references to words of knowledge. I pray you grow in your biblical understanding of how this gift has been used throughout God's Word.

1 SEEING A BREAKTHROUGH IN CIRCUMSTANCE

Acts 9:12: In a vision he has seen a man named Ananias come and place his hands on him to restore his sight.

2 REVEALING DESTINY

Acts 9:15-16: But the Lord said to Ananias, "Go! This man is my chosen instrument to proclaim my name to the Gentiles and their kings and to the people of Israel. I will show him how much he must suffer for my name."

3 MAKING DIVINE CONNECTIONS

Acts 10:19-20: While Peter was still thinking about the vision, the Spirit said to him, "Simon, three men are looking for you. So get up and go downstairs. Do not hesitate to go with them, for I have sent them."

4 KNOWING OTHERS' THOUGHTS AND INTENTIONS

Matthew 9:4-8: Knowing their thoughts, Jesus said, "Why do you entertain evil thoughts in your hearts? Which is easier: to say, 'Your sins are forgiven,' or to say, 'Get up and walk'? But I want you to know that the Son of Man has authority on earth to forgive sins." So he said to the paralyzed man, "Get up, take your mat and go home." Then the man got up and went home. When the crowd saw this, they were filled with awe; and they praised God, who had given such authority to man.

1 Corinthians 14:24-25: But if an unbeliever or an inquirer comes in while everyone is prophesying, they are convicted of sin and are brought under judgment by all, as the secrets of their hearts are laid bare. So they will fall down and worship God, exclaiming, "God is really among you!"

Luke 5:22: Jesus knew what they were thinking and asked, "Why are you thinking these things in your hearts?"

Mark 2:8: Immediately Jesus knew in his spirit that this was what they were thinking in their hearts, and he said to them, "Why are you thinking these things?"

Matthew 22:18: But Jesus, knowing their evil intent, said, "You hypocrites, why are you trying to trap me?"

CHAPTER SIX
TEACHING POINTS

1   God speaks to us in numerous and diverse ways.

I want to walk you through some of the many ways people hear from God so that you can learn to identify and even practice, or be aware of, how God wants to talk to you.

In our training, one of the most common questions people ask is, "Is it normal if I hear this way or that way?" There is no normal in God. We have no rules for how all of this works. He is the God who calls Himself the Creator. Can we really define an infinite God or put His process in a box? I love how Jesus never did the same two miracles the same way. We have a God who doesn't give us scientific formulas for success in relationship; instead, He gives us tools to make our relationship successful.

If you're looking for a relational process, you won't try to develop each of these tools as its own goal; you'll be open to trying new things and experimenting with a spectrum of gifts. You might say, "I don't have a developed imagination. I don't see pictures in my head." But then in your pursuit to hear God, you might primarily get pictures because He's working past your limitations. God works through our perceived weaknesses to bring glory to Himself and to share His love with others.

God gave us so many tools for helping us connect to revelation. If you're new to the whole subject of prophetic gifts, I want to help define these tools for you.

Tools and Types of Words of Knowledge:

Impressions
I believe this is the number-one way most people hear from God. It's the idea of having God download His thoughts or a picture into your mind.

NOTES

_____
_____
_____
_____
_____
_____
_____
_____
_____
_____
_____
_____
_____
_____
_____
_____
_____
_____
_____
_____
_____
_____

NOTES

Picture your smart device or computer equipment receiving its processor upgrade or an update. This is how our Spirit can work with God—something just downloads inside of us. We have an immediate thought that is as strong as if we had been thinking it our whole lives. In Mark's Gospel, he paints a word picture of Jesus being "aware in His Spirit":

Immediately Jesus, aware in His spirit that they were reasoning that way within themselves, said to them, "Why are you reasoning about these things in your hearts? Which is easier, to say to the paralytic, 'Your sins are forgiven'; or to say, 'Get up, and pick up your pallet and walk'? But so that you may know that the Son of Man has authority on earth to forgive sins"—He said to the paralytic, "I say to you, get up, pick up your pallet and go home." And he got up and immediately picked up the pallet and went out in the sight of everyone, so that they were all amazed and were glorifying God, saying, "We have never seen anything like this" (Mark 2:8).

Then he opened their minds so they could understand the Scriptures (Luke 24:45, NIV).

Visions
A vision happens when you receive a word picture, a mental image, a daydream realm visual, a full moving picture, an open picture, or an open visionary experience. The Bible is full of these kinds of experiences. It doesn't matter if it's a mental image you see in your head or an open vision outside of you that is as real as anything else you're seeing. They are both valuable. We often discount internal word pictures, but when we learn that God speaks to us or shows us things this way, we can find powerful connections through these visions.

And he has seen in a vision a man named Ananias come in and lay his hands on him, so that he might regain his sight (Acts 2:12).

During the night Paul had a vision of a man of Macedonia standing and begging him, "Come over to Macedonia and help us." After Paul had seen the vision, we got ready at once to leave for Macedonia, concluding that God had called us to preach the gospel to them (Acts 16:9-11, NIV).

Dreams

God sends many of our dreams through the Holy Spirit, and we can learn to interpret them. Sometimes dreams have direct ramifications, literally predicting the near or distant future, and sometimes they're parabolic. I've had dreams that helped reveal a situation in someone's past or current area of their life. These words of knowledge that come from spiritual dreams can be a great deposit inside of us.

> Now Joseph had a dream, and when he told it to his brothers they hated him even more. He said to them, "Hear this dream that I have dreamed: Behold, we were binding sheaves in the field, and behold, my sheaf arose and stood upright. And behold, your sheaves gathered around it and bowed down to my sheaf." His brothers said to him, "Are you indeed to reign over us? Or are you indeed to rule over us?" So they hated him even more for his dreams and for his words. Then he dreamed another dream and told it to his brothers and said, "Behold, I have dreamed another dream. Behold, the sun, the moon, and eleven stars were bowing down to me." But when he told it to his father and to his brothers, his father rebuked him and said to him, "What is this dream that you have dreamed? Shall I and your mother and your brothers indeed come to bow ourselves to the ground before you?" And his brothers were jealous of him, but his father kept the saying in mind (Genesis 37:5-11, ESV).

Trance

A trance happens when you experience a heightened spiritual awareness. You are more connected to God through the Spirit then you are to the world around you. It can be a dreamlike state when you're awake. During a trance, you can feel more connected to God's thoughts or emotions, and words of knowledge can flow freely here. One minor form of trance is the heightened focus we experience when we get caught up in worship music. Have you ever been in a time of worship where the whole room fades and any other thought about your life just disappears as you come into a state of affection and

NOTES

NOTES

adoration, thinking mostly or solely about God? This is that heightened state of awareness that can lead to revelation.

> Peter began speaking and proceeded to explain to them in orderly sequence, saying, "I was in the city of Joppa praying; and in a trance I saw a vision, an object coming down like a great sheet lowered by four corners from the sky; and it came right down to me" (Acts 11:4).

Direct Voice

Sometimes God just speaks. It can be His audible voice—the same as if someone else is talking and everyone can hear and understand what he's saying. It can also be a projected voice into your head that's beyond mere thoughts or inspired ideas. Some people use the phrase "telepathic voice" because it's a voice that starts internally in you and becomes external.

> Then a voice came out of the cloud, saying, "This is My Son, My Chosen One; listen to Him!" And when the voice had spoken, Jesus was found alone. And they kept silent, and reported to no one in those days any of the things which they had seen (Luke 9:35).

2   Internal dialogue requires us to know when we're hearing our thoughts vs. hearing God's thoughts.

Knowing your thoughts and separating them from God's thoughts is key. God speaks so much through inner dialogue. The more we know ourselves in a healthy way, the more we can discern the difference between our thoughts and God's. As you mature in your identity as a Christian, you'll get to know yourself really well. This creates inner emotional intelligence, which can then manifest itself in social intelligence as well.

Legalism and pride create very bad boundaries for our inner dialogue. Bad theology can come across as sovereign in our hearts (meaning that when you believe something, you give it power). If you believe the wrong thing, it will take away the power of the right thing. For example, if you're legalistic and think that you have to earn your way to God, the importance of grace diminishes. I think of how before Saul met Jesus on the road to Damascus, Saul the persecutor operated in pure legalism. When the scales fell off his eyes, his religious mindset was not just broken, but God created a new nature in him. In this new nature, Saul turned Paul was not only freed from the religious pressure nagging him in his inner thoughts, but also his mind was renewed. He could recognize when God was speaking or inspiring him versus when it was something that was just a great idea.

Let's put it this way: Have you ever been told something was wrong and that has jaded the way you relate to someone who does it? For instance, some Christians are convinced that it's better to not drink alcohol at all to set an example. As a result, when they see other Christians drink, it's upsetting to them. It would be hard to have a word for someone who owns a vineyard or restaurant that serves wine because your fundamental belief system is against their pursuit in the first place. You've made it a moral issue versus a personal issue. Your conscience could easily steer you away from God's thoughts just by default of legalism.

Our inner dialogue can also be incredibly amazing though. Our own thoughts can inspire us to ask God the biggest questions, which He desperately wants to answer. Our inner dialogue can birth great vision in our imagination for what is possible as God inspires our mind to creatively think past what we could hope for in our own ability.

So much of what God says lives right next to our own inner dialogue. We have to recognize the intertwining of His thoughts responding to our own.

3 Pressing in for a greater measure of the gift requires intentionality and practice.

Pursuing spiritual gifts is much like working out. It takes practice, intentionality, discipline, and fortitude. The more you exercise the gifts, the more you'll receive them. When I say that I didn't start out that gifted, people repeatedly ask me, "Can I really grow

NOTES

NOTES

_____
_____
_____
_____
_____
_____
_____
_____
_____
_____
_____
_____
_____
_____
_____
_____
_____
_____

in a significant way in words of knowledge?" My answer is always a resounding yes!

To grow in this gift, you must be intentional. Here are a few things I suggest you do:

(1) Listen to others who move in words of knowledge. Watch videos, go to events, watch Darren Wilson's movies and TV show. Watch our YouTube clips. Surround yourself with examples because faith comes through hearing. (2) Challenge yourself. Give yourself homework, and when you're getting good at one type of word of knowledge, up the ante! I compete with myself all of the time: *Tonight if I hear God, I'm going to press in for one more word of knowledge about each person I minister to than I originally received. I'm constantly out and about, and I will give myself a challenge: Try to love one person and know something really personal about their business.* Then I'll look for a businessperson and, lo and behold, I'll have the encounter I prayed for. (3) Study all of the types of words of knowledge outlined in this chapter, as well as all of the other biblical stories that demonstrate words of knowledge. Scripture creates the healthiest soil for the growth of your faith.

4 Setting a goal to be specific will help you grow in words of knowledge.

When we minister to people with the prophetic gifts, we're allowed to set an internal goal to display their secrets when it leads them to acknowledge God. This is what Paul spoke about in 1 Corinthians 14:25: "...as the secrets of their hearts are laid bare. So they will fall down and worship God, exclaiming, 'God is really among you!'"

Paul would have never given this instruction and set this goal if it wasn't possible. In our clinics, so many people have asked me if it's arrogant to go after specific words or if it's even "psychic." We are asking the God of all the universe who created everything and everyone to speak to us. It is inherently not arrogant because throughout Scripture He lays out His desire for a relationship with us. It would be stupid to think that our all-powerful God wants to be generic.

Many times when we're generic, it comes across as speaking in tongues, which doesn't really minister true spiritual encouragement because it doesn't deal with what is in a person's heart in the here and now.

I've actually grown quite a bit just by asking God questions about the person I'm ministering to. I have a four-step model that I teach people to use when they're learning how to receive revelation. We are allowed to ask God about someone when our motive is relationship with Him and seeing people connect to God. These are the four steps: (1) Ask God about their heart and life and what He loves about them. Why did He make them? (2) Ask God about their family and their friends and the relationships that are the most precious to them. (3) Ask God about their occupation or what they spend the most time doing. (4) Ask God about their spiritual calling and what God made them to do.

If you get any potential revelation from asking these questions, then it's time to ask even more questions. I might ask the first question and get nothing so I go on to the second question. On the second question, I may get an impression that this person is really concerned for a family member. Then I ask God the questions, "Who?" and "Why?" There's no guarantee that I'll hear or know anything else, but why not ask? We are wired for relationship; let's take this as far as we can. You can feel when the Holy Spirit stops talking because the tap will run dry.

I love how people in the Old Testament would go to the prophets because they knew that if the prophet got a revelation, it would be a huge game changer for their lives. We need to ask questions to know God's secrets.

NOTES

QUESTIONS FOR JOURNALING

1. What is the main way you hear from God right now? What are some of the most unique ways God has spoken and speaks to you?

_____
_____
_____
_____
_____
_____
_____
_____

2. Do you feel like your own internal dialog is healthy? Are you able to discern your thoughts from God's thoughts?

_____
_____
_____
_____
_____
_____
_____
_____
_____
_____

3. If you do prayer ministry sometimes for people, do you ask God questions to get more specific revelation?

Make a list of some personal homework assignments you can give yourself to press in for more.

_____
_____
_____
_____
_____
_____
_____
_____

 QUIZ

Instruction: Have you ever wondered what the difference is between a word of knowledge, word of wisdom, word of discernment, and prophecy? I encourage you to read the scriptures below, identify the gift the verse reflects, and circle the correct answer.

A contextual understanding of these gifts is available // *on page 127 - 128*
Answer key available // *on page 141*

1. Acts 9:11-16 (NASB)

"And the Lord said to him, 'Get up and go to the street called Straight, and inquire at the house of Judas for a man from Tarsus named Saul, for he is praying, and he has seen in a vision a man named Ananias come in and lay his hands on him, so that he might regain his sight.' But Ananias answered, 'Lord, I have heard from many about this man, how much harm he did to Your saints at Jerusalem; and here he has authority from the chief priests to bind all who call on Your name.' But the Lord said to him, 'Go, for he is a chosen instrument of Mine, to bear My name before the Gentiles and kings and the sons of Israel; for I will show him how much he must suffer for My name's sake.'"

a. WORD OF KNOWLEDGE   b. PROPHECY

c. DISCERNMENT   d. WORD OF WISDOM

2. Matthew 22:18 (NASB)

"But Jesus perceived their malice, and said, 'Why are you testing Me, you hypocrites?'"

a. WORD OF KNOWLEDGE   b. PROPHECY

c. DISCERNMENT   c. WORD OF WISDOM

3. Acts 10:23-29 (NASB)

"So he invited them in and gave them lodging. And on the next day he got up and went away with them, and some of the brethren from Joppa accompanied him. On the following day he entered Caesarea. Now Cornelius was waiting for them and had called together his relatives and close friends. When Peter entered, Cornelius met him, and fell at his feet and worshiped him. But Peter raised him up, saying, 'Stand up; I too am just a man.' As he talked with him, he entered and found many people assembled. And he said to them, 'You yourselves know how unlawful it is for a man who is a Jew to associate with a foreigner or to visit him; and yet God has shown me that I should not call any man unholy or unclean. That is why I came without even raising any objection when I was sent for. So I ask for what reason you have sent for me.'"

a. WORD OF KNOWLEDGE   b. PROPHECY

c. DISCERNMENT   d. WORD OF WISDOM

4. Acts 16:9-11 (NIV)

"During the night Paul had a vision of a man of Macedonia standing and begging him, 'Come over to Macedonia and help us.' After Paul had seen the vision, we got ready at once to leave for Macedonia, concluding that God had called us to preach the gospel to them. From Troas we put out to sea and sailed straight for Samothrace, and the next day we went on to Neapolis."

a. WORD OF KNOWLEDGE   b. PROPHECY

c. DISCERNMENT   d. WORD OF WISDOM

5. Nehemiah 6:10-14 (NASB)

"When I entered the house of Shemaiah the son of Delaiah, son of Mehetabel, who was confined at home, he said, 'Let us meet together in the house of God, within the temple, and let us close the doors of the temple, for they are coming to kill you, and they are coming to kill you at night.' But I said, 'Should a man like me flee? And could one such as I go into the temple to save his life? I will not go in.' Then I perceived that surely God had not sent him, but he uttered his prophecy against me because Tobiah and Sanballat had hired him. He was hired for this reason, that I might become frightened and act accordingly and sin, so that they might have an evil report in order that they could reproach me. Remember, O my God, Tobiah and Sanballat according to these works of theirs, and also Noadiah the prophetess and the rest of the prophets who were trying to frighten me."

a. WORD OF KNOWLEDGE   b. PROPHECY

c. DISCERNMENT   d. WORD OF WISDOM

INDIVIDUAL ACTIVITIES

RIGHT NOW RISK

Identify and write down how you hear or receive from God. Make a list of other ways you want to hear the Lord. Take time to talk to the Lord about those desires and ask Him to begin speaking to you in those new ways.

LIFESTYLE OPPORTUNITY

For each day this week, pick a person you're around and ask God about them, using the questions in the four-step model above. Write down any words of knowledge you feel you're getting. Now take the risk and ask them if any of it is correct. You can always qualify why you're doing this: "I'm doing a workshop on hearing God's voice, and I had some spiritual impressions I would like to share with you. Can I have two minutes?"

GROUP ACTIVITIES

Break up into small groups. We're going to focus on some of the ways God can speak through you. Ask God to speak words of knowledge about those in your group via your five senses. Start out by recognizing what you're currently *hearing, feeling* (both emotionally and physically), *smelling, tasting*, and actually *seeing*. Now ask the Holy Spirit to touch your senses. What do you feel, hear, smell, taste and see? As you feel aware of something different than what you originally perceived, ask God for details about the sensation. For example, maybe you hear a buzzing sound. It could be someone has buzzing in their ear. Maybe you smell a familiar perfume that wasn't familiar before, and it ends up being the favorite scent of the mother of the person you're ministering to. In other words, don't let yourself get boxed in and think, *This is how it works*. God will surprise you every time. He speaks to us in creative ways because He's a creative God.

Share as a group what you received for each other. Gather feedback.

▨ DISCUSSIONS

Discuss as a group how you each hear from God and take a census on all of the primary ways listed and described in this chapter. Now pray for each other to grow in new ways and ask God to activate it right now.

_____
_____
_____
_____
_____
_____
_____
_____
_____
_____
_____
_____
_____
_____
_____

 PRAYER

Lord, I love that You speak to me! I believe that You talk to me and love sharing Your secrets with me. I declare that I have ears to hear Your voice and eyes to see what You are doing. Will you please show me all of the different ways You make Yourself known to me? I will intentionally look for the ways you communicate with me. I ask for confirmation through different sources that I'm hearing You well. I also invite You, Lord, to speak to me in new ways. I give time to developing our relationship. I will take time to mature my ability to hear You and see You. I believe You speak and desire to share words of knowledge with me. *In Jesus' Name. Amen.*

 # WORD OF KNOWLEDGE TESTIMONY

Little Runner

Me: I heard the song lyric, "I think we're alone now..." so you must be Tiffany. Does that make sense?

Tiffany: Yes!

Me: Have you been married about nine years?

Tiffany/Husband: Eight years.

Me: You've been married eight years and are in my your ninth?

Tiffany/Husband: Yes!

Me: And you have three kids?

Tiffany/Husband: Yes!

Me: I hear the ninth year is the charm. It's going to be a really good year for you. Not just for you, but for your whole family. I kept seeing Troy Aikman or Clay Aiken. I was trying to figure out how to spell Clay Aiken, and I should have just looked it up! Is your last name Aiken?

Tiffany/Husband: Yes!

Me: God really wants to touch a Michael and a Jen, from Missouri, I think. Does that make sense?

Tiffany/Husband: Yes!

Me: They lost their little runner. Does that make sense?

Tiffany/Husband: Yes.

Me: Little runner had some sort of disease, degenerative disease? Muscle atrophy? Muscular dystrophy?

Tiffany/Husband (very emotional): Yes.

Me: Is this your brother or your cousin?

Husband: Cousin.

Me: God wants to show you that because of the choices you've made and how you have taken with Jesus, your whole family is going to be affected. It would be good for Michael and Jen to watch this video of us talking.

They have lost their little runner, but he's running with Jesus in heaven and he is with Dave's wife, Beverly. Hand in hand with Jesus. It's his grandfather. This is Michael's father.

Dave needs to hear this, too. He lost the love of his life in Beverly, but she has been praying every step of the way. She was a wonderful, wonderful woman and it broke his heart when she passed away and he hasn't been able to move on. She's been praying that he would get the rest of his destiny, get the rest of his life. Let him live again and that this season of grieving is over. It's time for him to live again. Beverly is crying out, "Live again, live again through Jesus."

This little scrapper who's left, this little boy who is left in their family, who's so awesome, who's like a little chase, chase, chase...

Tiffany: Dash.

Me: Dash...what a weird name! I love that name! Is the other brother's name literally Runner?

Tiffany: Runner and Dash.

Me: Oh my gosh! I just saw a little runner in heaven because they were all athletes. I didn't know his name was Runner. Dash is his younger brother. Dash has a champion call on his life to be seen and inspire. Father, touch Michael and Jen to raise Dash up with a healthy entitlement, that he can do anything he wants. The season of grieving is passing. This type of grief is passing as they hear that these ones are still alive in Christ. I can see them alive in Jesus. Runner is running. He couldn't run in life. He was bound in a wheelchair. He was such a happy kid. He was a joy to everyone, but it was such a hardship on your family.

God plucked out one part of your family today to show you that He is going to bring all of your family into their full purpose.

God bless you guys!

DELIVERY (SHARING GOD'S SECRETS)

"As each has received a gift, use it to serve one another, as good stewards of God's varied grace."

1 Peter 4:10

CHAPTER OVERVIEW

- ⬦ Invitation Scripture
- ⬦ Getting to Know Words of Knowledge
- ⬦ Three Teaching Points
- ⬦ Questions / Journal
- ⬦ Quiz
- ⬦ Individual Activities
  - ⬦ Right Now Risk
  - ⬦ Lifestyle Opportunity
- ⬦ Group Activities
- ⬦ Discussions
- ⬦ Prayer
- ⬦ Testimony

TEACHING POINTS

1 Sharing words of knowledge with others reveals God's heart toward them.

2 When sharing words of knowledge, put some guiding principles in place.

3 Remember the dos and don'ts of delivery.

GETTING TO KNOW WORDS OF KNOWLEDGE

Instruction: Read and prayerfully consider the following Scripture references to words of knowledge. I pray you grow in your biblical understanding of how this gift has been used throughout God's Word.

1 GIVING WARNINGS/PROVIDING SAFETY

Acts 27:10: Men, I can see that our voyage is going to be disastrous and bring great loss to ship and cargo, and to our own lives also.

2 Kings 6:9: The man of God sent word to the king of Israel: "Beware of passing that place, because the Arameans are going down there."

Matthew 2:12: And having been warned in a dream not to go back to Herod, they returned to their country by another route.

2 PREPARING EVANGELISM

John 4:17-26: "I have no husband," she replied. Jesus said to her, "You are right when you say you have no husband. The fact is, you have had five husbands, and the man you now have is not your husband. What you have just said is quite true." "Sir," the woman said, "I can see that you are a prophet. Our ancestors worshiped on this mountain, but you Jews claim that the place where we must worship is in Jerusalem." "Woman," Jesus replied, "believe me, a time is coming when you will worship the Father neither on this mountain nor in Jerusalem. You Samaritans worship what you do not know; we worship what we do know, for salvation is from the Jews. Yet a time is coming and has now come when the true worshipers will worship the Father in the Spirit and in truth, for they are the kind of worshipers the Father seeks. God is spirit, and his worshipers must worship in the Spirit and in truth." The woman said, "I know that Messiah" (called Christ) "is coming. When he comes, he will explain everything to us." Then Jesus declared, "I, the one speaking to you—I am he."

John 1:47-51: When Jesus saw Nathanael approaching, he said of him, "Here truly is an Israelite in whom there is no deceit." "How do you know me?" Nathanael asked. Jesus answered, "I saw you while you were still under the fig tree before Philip called you."

Then Nathanael declared, "Rabbi, you are the Son of God; you are the king of Israel." Jesus said, "You believe because I told you I saw you under the fig tree. You will see greater things than that." He then added, "Very truly I tell you, you will see 'heaven open, and the angels of God ascending and descending on' the Son of Man."

3 BREAKING SOCIETAL RESTRICTIONS (BIGOTRY AGAINST THE GENTILES)

Acts 10:9-27: The voice spoke to him a second time, "Do not call anything impure that God has made clean." This happened three times, and immediately the sheet

Getting to Know Words of Knowledge (Continued)

was taken back to heaven. While Peter was wondering about the meaning of the vision, the men sent by Cornelius found out where Simon's house was and stopped at the gate. They called out, asking if Simon who was known as Peter was staying there. While Peter was still thinking about the vision, the Spirit said to him, "Simon, three men are looking for you. So get up and go downstairs. Do not hesitate to go with them, for I have sent them." Peter went down and said to the men, "I'm the one you're looking for. Why have you come?" The men replied, "We have come from Cornelius the centurion. He is a righteous and God-fearing man, who is respected by all the Jewish people. A holy angel told him to ask you to come to his house so that he could hear what you have to say." Then Peter invited the men into the house to be his guests.

4 LOCATING PROVISION

Matthew 17:27: But so that we may not cause offense, go to the lake and throw out your line. Take the first fish you catch; open its mouth and you will find a four-drachma coin. Take it and give it to them for my tax and yours.

Matthew 21:2-3: Go to the village ahead of you, and at once you will find a donkey tied there, with her colt by her. Untie them and bring them to me. If anyone says anything to you, say that the Lord needs them, and he will send them right away.

CHAPTER SEVEN
TEACHING POINTS

1 Sharing words of knowledge with others reveals God's heart toward them.

So many people have read the Bible, but when it comes to actually hearing a word of knowledge for the first time, it causes awe or shock, or even skeptical questions such as "Did this person just research me? Is this for real?" We have to know the audience we're giving words to and really try to be sensitive to who they are and where they are in their lives and spiritual walk. That said, no one is ever "ready" to hear from God. It's such an otherworldly process!

I think about the times Jesus would bring revelation through all the examples we have used and how the person He would speak to would be utterly

NOTES

_____

_____

_____

_____

_____

_____

_____

_____

_____

_____

NOTES

amazed at the most basic of things: "I saw you sitting under a tree..." The response was always, "How do you know me?" People don't expect to be seen, heard or known. Have you ever had someone take a picture of you when you didn't know or expect it and then post it somewhere? Internet slang calls it to "ninja" someone, and it can be funny, fun or even scary when it happens to you.

When God gives you a word of knowledge for someone, you have a huge responsibility to deliver it appropriately. How you share what God is showing you is important because it's part of how you reveal His love and nature to someone. Jesus was the ultimate model of this. People He talked with and ministered to always felt the love of the Father through His example.

So here are some good questions to ask yourself when you're about to share something:

· Would I feel encouraged, edified or strengthened if someone shared this with me?
· Is this something that would potentially be helpful?
· Am I clear on what I'm going to try to say?
· Have I made the choice to value, honor, and love the person before I even speak?

Ultimately, we're supposed to help people connect with God. The Bible describes the Holy Spirit in a number of different ways: friend, counselor, comforter, etc. Ultimately, we're supposed to resemble this in all of our revelatory encounters with others.

2   When sharing words of knowledge, put some guiding principles in place.

As I've been growing in words of knowledge, I've come to realize there are some guiding themes that can help keep us on track. Here are four of those themes:

A. Use your discernment, but don't stop there. In my book *God Secrets*, I go into great detail discussing the difference between discernment and words of knowledge. We can discern negative things, sin, and even facts about someone, but the difference between that and prophecy is what God thinks about these facts or this knowledge. Words of knowledge offer us glimpses into the mind and heart of God that discernment doesn't always bring. Discernment is a conversation starter with God. It is an intercession and prayer device. It helps us avoid hard situations or navigate them. But it is not a prophecy. Still, it can help us. Make sure that the words you're getting from God are a helpful word of knowledge, not discernment.

B. Heaven has an agenda: to love. This is more important than trying to be right or going after accuracy of information. You're in a conversation between God and a person, trying to translate His heart.

C. Gain emotional intelligence and people skills beyond your comfort zone. If you want to be effective in really relating God's heart to people, learn the art of connection. The Holy Spirit can relate to all people at all times but can be so limited if we're small-minded, isolated, have a lack of emotional development, or live in a traumatized state. The more we grow in this gift, the larger the landing strip of experience gets. We continue to give Him room to breathe on us, helping us relate to His heart in the world around us. I think about Jesus who was born in Bethlehem, spent time in Egypt, moved to Nazareth, and then traveled all around. What He must have seen compared to others who barely made a pilgrimage outside of their own town! He related to people who weren't just those He had chemistry with; He was about the ones the Father loves. Most of us only know how to relate to people with whom we have much in common. A small few of us have friends who are not like us. If you're going to be effective in the Kingdom, you have to get outside yourself.

D. Learn to borrow the affection you feel for your close friends and family and then apply it to strangers. Introductions are awkward most of the time. All of us need a little time to warm up to someone we don't know, especially if he or she is outside our normal context. One of the ways we can learn to be sensitive is to apply the affection we have for someone we love to the person to whom we're trying to minister. We can borrow the feeling of "What if this was my sister? What if this was my son? What if this was like

NOTES

NOTES

Billy from work?" and then apply the feeling of love and affection we have for those people to the person we're with at the time. When you're about to minister to someone, this kind of relational transference helps you be more engaged with more skin in the game than if you rely on just spiritual impressions and intellectual choice. When you engage your heart and emotions, you'll always have a different result. A lot of people don't like this step. Rejection can hurt physically, mentally and spiritually. We tend to want to stay unengaged emotionally so that we can self-protect. But part of the beauty of the prophetic is the emotional side of the journey.

3 Remember the dos and don'ts of delivery.

The dos and don'ts of prophetic ministry with words of knowledge are easy:

- Don't assume the person will fully understand what you're saying. Instead, ask for confirmation or ask him/her to let you know if what you're telling him/her makes sense.
- Don't try to fix your words to make them work. If you asked someone if their birthdate was in June and it was in August, don't try to justify why you were off. Just accept it and move on.
- Don't put the pressure of interpreting what you're trying to say or see on the individual you're ministering to. Pause if you have to and really press in so that you're as clear as you can possibly be.
- Don't try to have more than you currently have. Sometimes we're uncomfortable with the limit of words or information that God has shared with us; or we might get confirmation from the individual about part of our word. At that point, we just want to speak more into it. And yet God was done speaking about it through us. Know when to stop talking. If you're a gabber, make sure to use fewer words, not more.
- Do share as fully as possible with someone as you're processing any words.
- Do ask God for more each time you seem to get something right. As your faith grows, He will often expound upon something in the encounter.
- Do get feedback and completely listen to someone before trying to respond. Don't necessarily give feedback in return.
- Do turn your love on as completely as you know how because it is the currency of revelation.

QUESTIONS FOR JOURNALING

1. Have you ever heard someone give a word that felt more like discernment than a word of knowledge? Have you ever given your discernment as a word?

_____
_____
_____
_____
_____
_____
_____

2. Define an experience in which someone was praying for you and it just connected—not just the word but also the person who delivered the word. Did you ever have a bad experience in which it felt like the word wasn't accurate or the person delivering it had a negative impact on you or caused confusion? Can you identify what that person should have done differently?

_____
_____
_____
_____
_____
_____
_____
_____

3. Has there ever been a time when you've received a wrong word of knowledge but it was given from a place of love? How did it make you feel? What impact did the moment have?

_____
_____
_____
_____
_____
_____
_____

 QUIZ

Instruction: Have you ever wondered what the difference is between a word of knowledge, word of wisdom, word of discernment, and prophecy? I encourage you to read the scriptures below, identify the gift the verse reflects, and circle the correct answer.

A contextual understanding of these gifts is available // *on page 127 - 128*
Answer key available // *on page 141*

1. Isaiah 9:6-7 (NASB)

"For a child will be born to us, a son will be given to us; And the government will rest on His shoulders; And His name will be called Wonderful Counselor, Mighty God, Eternal Father, Prince of Peace. There will be no end to the increase of His government or of peace, On the throne of David and over his kingdom, to establish it and to uphold it with justice and righteousness from then on and forevermore. The zeal of the LORD of hosts will accomplish this."

    a. WORD OF KNOWLEDGE   b. PROPHECY

    c. DISCERNMENT   d. WORD OF WISDOM

2. Acts 10:22 (NASB)

"They said, 'Cornelius, a centurion, a righteous and God-fearing man well spoken of by the entire nation of the Jews, was divinely directed by a holy angel to send for you to come to his house and hear a message from you.'"

    a. WORD OF KNOWLEDGE   b. PROPHECY

    c. DISCERNMENT   c. WORD OF WISDOM

3. Acts 10:34 (NASB)

"Opening his mouth, Peter said, 'I most certainly understand now that God is not one to show partiality.'"

    a. WORD OF KNOWLEDGE   b. PROPHECY

    c. DISCERNMENT   d. WORD OF WISDOM

4. 1 Kings 19:14-18 (NASB)

"Then he said, 'I have been very zealous for the Lord, the God of hosts; for the sons of Israel have forsaken Your covenant, torn down Your altars and killed Your prophets with the sword. And I alone am left; and they seek my life, to take it away.' The Lord said to him, 'Go, return on your way to the wilderness of Damascus, and when you have arrived, you shall anoint Hazael king over Aram; and Jehu the son of Nimshi you shall anoint king over Israel; and Elisha the son of Shaphat of Abel-meholah you shall anoint as prophet in your place. It shall come about, the one who escapes from the sword of Hazael, Jehu shall put to death, and the one who escapes from the sword of Jehu, Elisha shall put to death. Yet I will leave 7,000 in Israel, all the knees that have not bowed to Baal and every mouth that has not kissed him.'"

    a. WORD OF KNOWLEDGE   b. PROPHECY

    c. DISCERNMENT   d. WORD OF WISDOM

5. Acts 15:19-22 (NASB)

"'Therefore, it is my judgment that we do not trouble those who are turning to God from among the Gentiles, but that we write to them that they abstain from things contaminated by idols and from fornication and from what is strangled and from blood. For Moses from ancient generations has in every city those who preach him, since he is read in the synagogues every Sabbath.' Then it seemed good to the apostles and the elders, with the whole church, to choose men from among them to send to Antioch with Paul and Barnabas—Judas called Barsabbas, and Silas, leading men among the brethren."

    a. WORD OF KNOWLEDGE   b. PROPHECY

    c. DISCERNMENT   d. WORD OF WISDOM

INDIVIDUAL ACTIVITIES

RIGHT NOW RISK

If the prophetic can be the most powerful through you with people whom you love deeply, then let's try to get a word for one! Spend some time with God in prayer and ask for a word of knowledge for a friend or family member. Call that person or deliver it to him/her through a face-to-face experience (not text or email, so pick someone with whom you can speak directly). Invite that friend or family member to give you feedback on your delivery of the word of knowledge.

· Did he/she feel that God loved him/her based on the word?
· Did you use easy-to-understand terminology?
· Did you overshare or share inappropriately?

· Was the person to whom you ministered able to relate to what you were saying?
· Was the word believable and delivered with confidence?

LIFESTYLE OPPORTUNITY

Choose a person outside of your Christian experience (he is unsaved or comes from a non-charismatic background or church where they don't practice the prophetic). Every day, call and pray for that person. Ask him if you can pray for him and for what he needs specific prayer. Then tell him that you're going to ask God to do it for him right there, and that in the days ahead, you'll also share anything you feel like God shows you. Pray and share.

 GROUP ACTIVITIES

Break up into small groups. Ask each person to take a turn prophesying over one other person in your group in front of everyone. After you're finished prophesying, get feedback from the person over whom you prophesied. Now, after the feedback and having more information from the person, ask God for more about what you were prophesying. (This shows you how to press into God for more once you have some level of information or discernment on how to use it.) Have the group do another round of prophesying, but the second time around, other individuals can contribute any words of knowledge they get with the initial person prophesying.

 # DISCUSSIONS

Talk about the difference between discernment and revelation. Let's clear up any confusion between the two!

_____

_____

_____

_____

_____

_____

_____

_____

_____

_____

_____

_____

_____

_____

_____

 # PRAYER

Lord, I'm so excited that I'm learning to hear You speak to me! I have learned and experienced the importance of delivery when giving a word of knowledge. I'm ready to share what You have spoken to me. Will You train me how to deliver Your words well to others? I ask that You would teach me how to share words of knowledge out of a place of love. I declare right now that love will be the foundation from which I deliver any and all words. I commit to asking You, Holy Spirit, how to best deliver the words of knowledge You give to me. I'm open to developing my delivery of words of knowledge and ask for opportunities to grow in this area. Lord, I believe You will lead me when I share Your secrets with others. *In Jesus' Name. Amen.*

WORD OF KNOWLEDGE TESTIMONY

Bill Johnson

At a meeting at Bethel Church in Redding California:
Me: It was like I was seeing two places at once. I was in heaven seeing Bob Jones. I'm not sure if it was literal or parabolic. I saw him talking to someone. I was looking at the person—the person he was talking to. I saw a map, and I saw that you take Olive Street, then turn right onto Gold Street, then turn right onto Oakridge Street. Does this make sense to anyone?

Bill Johnson (in the front row of Bethel): My mother lives on Oakridge Street.

I repeat the map I see.

Bill confirms it's accurate.

Me: God is talking to someone. I know your dad's name is Earl, but this guy's name is Melvin.

Bill: My dad's name is Melvin Earl Johnson.

Me: Wow! Your dad is Melvin Earl Johnson. So Bob Jones and your dad are talking with each other. It was a Bob Jones-type of word. Olive Street symbolizes the anointing to press the olives into wine, then you have to go down Gold Street and I saw your dad and he lives on Gold Street now. This symbolizes your need for the resources and the anointing that will produce the resources in this next season. This will get you to Oakridge Street that symbolizes a deep new wineskin of a move of long-term generational oaks. There is a release of great provision that's coming out of the anointing to plant the oaks—oaks of righteousness.

This is parabolic, and I can't explain it, but, Bill, you will get it. The anointing will produce the gold to produce the oaks of righteousness. Bob and your dad are talking about this right now over us in a leadership room—over Bethel Church and over Redding. This next move and installment from the Lord will land and superimpose over us. Your dad is the greatest intercessor, and he and Bob are in intercession to bring this purpose.

FAITH

"That the God of our Lord Jesus Christ, the Father of glory, may give unto you the spirit of wisdom and revelation in the knowledge of him."

Ephesians 1:17

CHAPTER OVERVIEW

- ☐ Invitation Scripture
- ☐ Getting to Know Words of Knowledge
- ☐ Two Teaching Points
- ☐ Questions / Journal
- ☐ Quiz
- ☐ Individual Activities
  - ☐ Right Now Risk
  - ☐ Lifestyle Opportunity
- ☐ Group Activities
- ☐ Discussions
- ☐ Prayer
- ☐ Testimony

TEACHING POINTS

1   Our capacity is limited so that we have to ensure we're filling ourselves with faith, not fear.

2   Believing that God will use you to share His heart requires an intentional process.

GETTING TO KNOW WORDS OF KNOWLEDGE

Instruction: Read and prayerfully consider the following Scripture references to words of knowledge. I pray you grow in your biblical understanding of how this gift has been used throughout God's Word.

1   PROVIDING TRANSPORTATION

Acts 8:26-40: The Ethiopian's chariot ride

Luke 19:30-31: Go to the village ahead of you, and as you enter it, you will find a colt tied there, which no one has ever ridden. Untie it and bring it here. If anyone asks you, "Why are you untying it?" say, "The Lord needs it."

2   PASSING OF DICTATOR

Matthew 2:19-20: After Herod died, an angel of the Lord appeared in a dream to Joseph in Egypt and said, "Get up, take the child and his mother and go to the land of Israel, for those who were trying to take the child's life are dead."

3   PASSING OF SELF

2 Peter 1:13-14: I think it is right to refresh your memory as long as I live in the tent of this body, because I know that I will soon put it aside, as our Lord Jesus Christ has made clear to me.

4   CHOOSING A SUCCESSOR

1 Kings 19:15-16: The Lord said to him, "Go back the way you came, and go to the Desert of Damascus. When you get there, anoint Hazael king over Aram. Also, anoint Jehu son of Nimshi king over Israel, and anoint Elisha son of Shaphat from Abel Meholah to succeed you as prophet."

CHAPTER EIGHT
TEACHING POINTS

1 Our capacity is limited so that we have to ensure we're filling ourselves with faith, not fear.

God created you with a huge capacity to grow in faith for Him to move in your life and through you as a person. He has given you a "container" that you can fill with faith, which operates as the currency of divine interactions between you and heaven. All the best things in God require this currency of faith in Him and who He is. If you fill this container, or capacity, with faith, you'll start to see more and more substance of God manifesting in your life and in your relationships. If you fill this container with fear, unbelief, wrong doctrine, and negativity, you won't be able to build a full measure of faith because, as a human, your capacity does have a limit. There is only so much space, so we have to focus on keeping our minds on whatever is pure, right, lovely, true—these will keep us at optimal peak status to be a conduit of God's heart and spiritual favor.

> For the Spirit God gave us does not make us timid, but gives us power, love and self-discipline (2 Timothy 1:7).

> But He said to them, "I have food to eat that you know nothing about" (John 4:32).

With words of knowledge, whenever you have agreed with unbelief or partnered with fear, this actually creates a block toward receiving revelation because it stands in the same place as where the revelation would have come. If you have hatred toward a people group, that hatred occupies the same place that God's Word and heart want to sit. If you have fear toward something, that fear will eat up that place of potential faith in which you want to grow. Again, we are limited by our capacity. We only have capacity for so much, whether that's encouragement and revelation or discouragement and fear.

NOTES

As Christians, there are countless scriptures about moral purity, keeping our heart soft and pure, faithfulness, and focusing on what is good and right. These are not just good themes or right principles. They are actually God-given guardrails that allow us to live out of a full capacity of faith. We limit ourselves to whatever we fill ourselves with. If we fill ourselves with fear, faith has no space. If we fill ourselves with hope, then faith has no limits.

2 Believing that God will use you to share His heart requires an intentional process.

We can grow in our faith that God will move in us by surrounding ourselves with God's stories. Living a life plugged into what He has done both through the Word and in others, as well as in ourselves, is essential!

Growing in faith takes an intentional process; no one grows by mistake. Just as our bodies require food and water to grow, so too we have to nourish our faith. Faith comes by

- Hearing stories and testimonies (see Romans 10:17)
- Imagining (see Ephesians 3:20)
- Taking risks (see 2 Timothy 1:7)
- Being a positive person (see Philippians 4:13)
- Cultivating a very active prayer life with prayers that are answerable on your prayer list (see John 15:7)
- Tracking what God is doing in your life and re minding yourself of these testimonies and stories (see Deuteronomy 8:2)

Make an ongoing list of your stories!

QUESTIONS FOR JOURNALING

1. How is your faith capacity? Is it full of faith or something else? Try to define the good and try to define feelings of fear, anxiety or unbelief. What is a process you can pursue to help you live a balanced healthy capacity of faith?

_____
_____
_____
_____
_____
_____
_____
_____
_____
_____

2. Has fear ever blocked your ability to receive clear revelation or have bold faith toward something?

_____
_____
_____
_____
_____
_____
_____
_____
_____
_____

3. What do you believe you would see happen in the area of words of knowledge if your faith were to increase?

_____
_____
_____
_____
_____
_____
_____
_____
_____

 QUIZ

Instruction: Have you ever wondered what the difference is between a word of knowledge, word of wisdom, word of discernment, and prophecy? I encourage you to read the scriptures below, identify the gift the verse reflects, and circle the correct answer.

A contextual understanding of these gifts is available // *on page 127 - 128*
Answer key available // *on page 141*

1. Acts 10:1-6 (ESV)

"At Caesarea there was a man named Cornelius, a centurion of what was known as the Italian Cohort, a devout man who feared God with all his household, gave alms generously to the people, and prayed continually to God. About the ninth hour of the day, he saw clearly in a vision an angel of God come in and say to him, 'Cornelius.' And he stared at him in terror and said, 'What is it, Lord?' And he said to him, 'Your prayers and your alms have ascended as a memorial before God. And now send men to Joppa and bring one Simon who is called Peter. He is lodging with one Simon, a tanner, whose house is by the sea.'"

    a. WORD OF KNOWLEDGE   b. PROPHECY

    c. DISCERNMENT   d. WORD OF WISDOM

2. Acts 6:2-6 (NASB)

"So the twelve summoned the congregation of the disciples and said, 'It is not desirable for us to neglect the word of God in order to serve tables. Therefore, brethren, select from among you seven men of good reputation, full of the Spirit and of wisdom, whom we may put in charge of this task. But we will devote ourselves to prayer and to the ministry of the word.' The statement found approval with the whole congregation; and they chose Stephen, a man full of faith and of the Holy Spirit, and Philip, Prochorus, Nicanor, Timon, Parmenas and Nicolas, a proselyte from Antioch. And these they brought before the apostles; and after praying, they laid their hands on them."

    a. WORD OF KNOWLEDGE   b. PROPHECY

    c. DISCERNMENT   c. WORD OF WISDOM

3. Luke 1:11-12 (NASB)

"And an angel of the Lord appeared to him, standing to the right of the altar of incense. Zacharias was troubled when he saw the angel, and fear gripped him."

a. WORD OF KNOWLEDGE   b. PROPHECY

c. DISCERNMENT   d. WORD OF WISDOM

4. Genesis 37:5-11 (NIV)

"Joseph had a dream, and when he told it to his brothers, they hated him all the more. He said to them, 'Listen to this dream I had: We were binding sheaves of grain out in the field when suddenly my sheaf rose and stood upright, while your sheaves gathered around mine and bowed down to it.' His brothers said to him, 'Do you intend to reign over us? Will you actually rule us?' And they hated him all the more because of his dream and what he had said. Then he had another dream, and he told it to his brothers. 'Listen,' he said, 'I had another dream, and this time the sun and moon and eleven stars were bowing down to me.' When he told his father as well as his brothers, his father rebuked him and said, 'What is this dream you had? Will your mother and I and your brothers actually come and bow down to the ground before you?' His brothers were jealous of him, but his father kept the matter in mind."

a. WORD OF KNOWLEDGE   b. PROPHECY

c. DISCERNMENT   d. WORD OF WISDOM

5. John 4:4-26 (NASB)

"And He had to pass through Samaria. So He came to a city of Samaria called Sychar, near the parcel of ground that Jacob gave to his son Joseph; and Jacob's well was there. So Jesus, being wearied from His journey, was sitting thus by the well. It was about the sixth hour. There came a woman of Samaria to draw water. Jesus said to her, 'Give Me a drink.' For His disciples had gone away into the city to buy food. Therefore the Samaritan woman said to Him, 'How is it that You, being a Jew, ask me for a drink since I am a Samaritan woman?' (For Jews have no dealings with Samaritans.) Jesus answered and said to her, 'If you knew the gift of God, and who it is who says to you, "Give Me a drink," you would have asked Him, and He would have given you living water.' She said to Him, 'Sir, You have nothing to draw with and the well is deep; where then do You get that living water? You are not greater than our father Jacob, are You, who gave us the well, and drank of it himself and his sons and his cattle?' Jesus answered and said to her, 'Everyone who drinks of this water that I will give him

Quiz (Continued)

shall never thirst; but the water that I will give him will become in him a well of water springing up to eternal life.' The woman said to Him, 'Sir, give me this water, so I will not be thirsty nor come all the way here to draw.' He said to her, 'Go, call your husband and come here.' The woman answered and said, 'I have no husband.' Jesus said to her, 'You have correctly said, "I have no husband"; for you have had five husbands, and the one whom you now have is not your husband; this you have said truly.' The woman said to Him, 'Sir, I perceive that You are a prophet. Our fathers worshiped in this mountain, and you people say that in Jerusalem is the place where men ought to worship.' Jesus said to her, 'Woman, believe Me, an hour is coming when neither in this mountain nor in Jerusalem will you worship the Father. You worship what you do not know; we worship what we know, for salvation is from the Jews. But an hour is coming, and now is, when the true worshipers will worship the Father in spirit and truth; for such people the Father seeks to be His worshipers. God is spirit, and those who worship Him must worship in spirit and truth.' The woman said to Him, 'I know that Messiah is coming (He who is called Christ); when that One comes, He will declare all things to us.' Jesus said to her, 'I who speak to you am He.'"

a. WORD OF KNOWLEDGE   b. PROPHECY

c. DISCERNMENT   d. WORD OF WISDOM

 INDIVIDUAL ACTIVITIES

 RIGHT NOW RISK

Write down a prophetic word for a leader in your church or community. It can be your pastor, a policeman, a city council member, a teacher, etc. Try to get at least one word of knowledge for him or her. Now email, text, or even snail mail it. Try to get feedback.

 LIFESTYLE OPPORTUNITY

Each day this week, try to give a word of knowledge to one person who has a leadership role in their environment (the manager at the coffee shop, a policewoman, a CEO of a company, the head of the PTA, a leader of a department at your church).

⟁ GROUP ACTIVITIES

Ask God individually for words of knowledge. Write down what you hear in the five categories mentioned below. After you complete your list, break up into groups and practice. Let's see how your words can affect the world around you.

1. Name of person (five names)
2. Locations (five possible locations)
3. Identifying characteristics: e.g., blue shirt, flamingo hat, red key chain (five characteristics)
4. Possible prayer needs: e.g., healing in shoulder, salvation, prayer for sibling (five needs)
5. Unique and random: anything that you feel might be a word of knowledge but you don't know where to put it (five areas)

💬 DISCUSSIONS

Do you have an internal rating system for words of knowledge? What areas of this gift do you feel more confident in giving (healing words, time tables in people's lives, words about family, words about someone's business, words about ministry calling or gifts, etc).

In which of the core values we went through do you sense the greatest need for growth? What are some intentional steps you can take to grow in this area?

_____
_____
_____
_____
_____
_____
_____
_____
_____
_____
_____
_____

PRAYER

Lord, increase my faith! I see the importance of having bold faith when giving words of knowledge. I ask that You bring me to new levels of faith. I partner with You by choosing to believe in the things You say and do. I desire to be known as a man/woman of faith. I ask that you teach me how to walk with boldness and surety in the things You have said. I ask, Lord, that my faith would change the atmosphere around me and encourage others to grow in their own faith and relationship with You. May this faith be infectious! I believe I can walk in faith because of who You are. You are faithful. *In Jesus' Name. Amen.*

WORD OF KNOWLEDGE TESTIMONY

Joy Zipper

I had never heard of Shawn and was actually at this meeting hoping for another prophetic word that had been spoken over my business at a Heaven in Business conference about a month prior. I was there to find answers. For years, I was a prophecy magnet. I had been called out and led by God through a series of prophetic words—not just this one. They are all unique and yet very much connected to each other. The difference with Shawn's word is that it was spoken on such a huge platform. All of my other words were primarily just between me and God. This was a whole new ballgame, and I knew I'd be facing some critics and skeptics. Hopefully, this will help everyone understand that you cannot judge another person's word. Only the person receiving it can judge the word.

Shawn said, "Is there, I don't know, I don't get this, but a Joy from, Joy from Germany? Or Berlin? That's what I saw. Joy from Berlin. Does that make sense? Are you Joy?"

I am.

"Are you from Berlin?"

Yes.

"But you're not German,"

I'm from Berlin, Ohio.

"Oh, that's cool. Berlin, Ohio, I didn't know there was one. This is really special. You're living in San Francisco."

Berlin, Ohio, is home to the largest Amish community in the world. My dad was born and raised Old Order Amish. To go from Berlin to San Francisco was mind-blowing to me. From that point on, Shawn had my full attention.

"This is good," Shawn said. "Um...I'm just looking down because I'm nervous. I'm trying to get the rest of this. I'm trying to get more. November...wow! November 9, 2010. John...this is your father, and he went to be with Jesus."

Oh man, are you kidding me? Did he actually just say November 9? Was God actually going to expose the greatest pain in my life on such a huge platform? The relationship I had with my dad was by far the most complicated one of my life. At times, we were each other's greatest adversaries and at times each other's greatest allies. My entire life I struggled to make sense of it, and after his death I had to accept it for what it was. Or so I thought.

"He was a prophet—John Shock?"

Yes, he was a prophet.

Looking back, I'm still blown away I actually said that out loud. I probably wouldn't have had I not been at a prophetic conference. I was still struggling to come to terms with the fact that my dad held the office of a prophet and never spoke a word of it to our family. It was a big deal. Why wouldn't he have told any of us? The first I heard of him being a prophet was from a prophetic word that was called in by another prophet, Dennis Peacocke from California. He spoke over my dad at the exact moment he took his last breath: "God gives us pioneers in every generation," Peacocke said. "He gives us spiritual fathers in every generation. He gives us prophets in every generation. When they go home, we then realize who they are by the legacy they leave. Eternity, move over! One such man is coming. Those of us left behind say thank you, thank you, thank you, John. Your work of prayer has now begun."

"I'm seeing him right now in heaven but he's behind you in heaven—like Jesus and your dad are behind you—and he's smiling and Jesus is saying, 'Write the book.'"

I gasp.

"Write the book. It's about his life. He has crazy stories, crazy. He's just a funny crazy man who has a story to be told. It's like a hodgepodge collection of just who he was and what he prophesied."

Ten weeks prior to my dad's stroke, I was in Ohio for five weeks for business and my daughter's wedding. I stayed at my mom and dad's house, which I never did when I came home for a visit. Several days prior to leaving, I had a conversation with my dad about writing a book on his life. My husband kept insisting that I write one, and I was highly annoyed because for once in my life I just wanted to enjoy my dad as just my dad. His persistence led to a discussion of what this book would include. My favorite stories were the ones where my dad would give a prophetic word and the word would come true. I can't tell you how many times I personally witnessed that happening. My dad was quite a character. He was larger than life. He was fearless, and his faith in God was beyond anything I've ever witnessed, which made for some incredible stories. We never really came to a clear conclusion about the content of the book.

"And I feel like the Lord is saying to you that it's an opportunity because your dad is literally praying over you and your husband who is also close to your dad, 'Notice the words.' Your dad is literally praying over you and your husband. Notice the words at his death: 'Your work of prayer has now begun.' Your husband really respected your dad. I can see this."

My husband is Jewish, and he adored my dad. My dad challenged his belief system in the simplest ways, and it rocked my husband's intellectual world. Three months after this word was spoken, my husband accepted Yeshua as his Savior and was baptized. He's been all in ever since.

"God is about to do something for you and your family," Shawn said, "and your dad is praying in heaven but there is a story to be told and you're going to be on a learning journey as you tell the story for how to tell greater and greater stories. You're going to steward something with God that's going to cause stewardship over your life."

As I've gathered the stories for the book, God has taken me on a journey of much-needed healing. I honestly thought I was fine. I had put the past behind me and was having so much fun with God. But as I was writing the book, I'd get stuck writing any part that I had not yet forgiven or did not yet understand. This forced me to dig deeper and seek out God in a deeper way than I ever had before. I feel like I've learned more in the last two years of my life than all of the years of my life combined. In many ways, my own story is being rewritten.

There is indeed a story to be told. The book will contain stories of my dad as a pastor, prophet, evangelist, entrepreneur and father—through my eyes and through my life story.

"I see your dad in all his glory. He looks around 30 years old. He looks so healthy; he's really fit, like he would have been at that age, and I feel like he's so happy with Jesus right now. Like I'm seeing that Jesus and he are best buddies. This man had the gift of gab, and he's talking Jesus' ear off all the time, and its Jesus' pleasure to have him there. It's so awesome."

After my dad's death, I had a picture made of him sitting on a bench beside Jesus. I had made these as a gift for the people who took over the ministry that he founded called LaRed. Shawn's words perfectly described my dad in that picture. We all know that my dad is talking Jesus' ear off. All of us knew that he could not wait to get to heaven to talk to Jesus about things that he had not in life found the answers to. My dad was always all in! His life was lived entirely to help usher in the Kingdom. It didn't matter if times were good or tough. He never lost his faith in God.

"But your dad is talking to Jesus about you and your husband and about your family and about your time in San Francisco, which is a divine assignment. There are some things you have to do there, and there are some things that you have to become. Your dad is part of your intercessory team."

I've always known that my landing in San Francisco was not an accident. There was never a question in my mind. It sure is nice to have confirmation. I've been having the most incredible supernatural experiences now for nearly six years. I'm still unclear about what the divine assignment actually is, but I no longer worry about it. I know if I stay in motion and stay focused on Him, He will make it clear when the time is right. For right now, my job is to finish writing this book.

"So just know that you're surrounded. I could tell that was so painful for you—but it's now a celebration day because your dad is still alive. He's alive in heaven right now. Bless you. Wow. Those are holy moments, right?"

Montell and Ginger

I was at Azusa Now and got the names Montell and Ginger and I knew that they were a couple. It turned out that Montell was at the event but was outside eating. When he came back inside, I asked him about several things I had seen: I saw their anniversary on November 8 and got the scripture Hebrews 11:7. I heard that they had chosen each other well and that they had met through the music industry. I also believed Ginger had done administrative work for him. Montell confirmed all the above but that their anniversary date was November 7. I remember saying, "At least I got Hebrews 11:7."

I then shared with them what the Lord had shared with me: "I saw God hovered over you both at the beach. This was when you first started dating. God says you have chosen well and he is blessing your marriage. The Lord showed me He loves to speak to Ginger through water. He also wants to communicate that your life as a hip-hop artist is not winding down but winding up. He is going to take you into a season of how to grow in this industry. This is not just for you, but also for Ginger's son whom you adopted through your marriage. There is something with music on his life. Montell, the Lord is going to visit your heart to show you He loves your music more than you do and that He loves your passions more than you do. He will affirm you in the deepest ways. I see you and Ginger as a signpost to people here today who are tired but they can now believe that the greater measure is coming.

Montell and Ginger (feedback via their Youtube video)

The week before Azusa Now, I was telling my wife that I wanted out. I told the Lord if You don't want me out of this marriage, then radically change something. I was eating outside and started receiving text messages and calls from people telling me that Shawn Bolz had just called Ginger and myself out by name. When I got back inside, he had shared Hebrews 11:7 and asked if November 8 was our anniversary. It was actually November 7. He spoke directly to our current struggle with our marriage, telling me that God said you chose right. He also talked about the influence of music in our life and marriage. We met through the music industry and Ginger did in fact do admin for me (like Shawn said). Shawn also said our first two dates were at the beach and that we fasted to see if we were supposed to be in a relationship.

"The Lord spoke to both of them," Shawn said, "saying that He would bless them if they remained single or got in a relationship. Love is a choice."

Shawn talked about Ginger's son and his calling in music. This is the son I adopted. He is very gifted in music. Since a young age, he could memorize and mimic songs. At the age of seven, he now fluently speaks Spanish. Shawn also spoke to the fact that God really does speak to Ginger through water. We also discovered that we were a signpost that day to many others whose faith was renewed because of what they saw.

DEFINITIONS

Definitions of Prophecy, Word of Knowledge, Word of Wisdom,
and Discernment

PROPHECY

Prophecy is a word about the future that shows the plans that God has for someone or a group/region/business, etc. With prophecy, people's affections lie in the fact that God knows them and has plans for them. Knowing God's plans and future for their lives gives people the opportunity to partner with Him to actually see those plans fulfilled. Simply put, prophecy is a love-based gift from the heart of God that pertains to the future context of a person, place or thing. History can inspire prophecy, but prophecy doesn't lend itself to identifying historical events. When you think about prophecy, think *future* context.

WORD OF KNOWLEDGE

One of three revelatory gifts cited in the Bible, a word of knowledge includes supernatural revelation by the Holy Spirit about something that's important to God. While not solely discerned, the information includes specific facts that will help bring God's knowledge through a manifest form into your life or into the life of someone you're ministering to and sharing God's heart. Word of knowledge is a divine knowing of a fact about a person, place, thing or situation that's in the past or present. It can also be a fragment of knowledge God gives to an individual. A word of knowledge cannot originate from an already known fact or from research.

WORD OF WISDOM

Word of wisdom is God-inspired application for a given person, place, thing, or situation. It is divine instruction: how to and how God would. Contextually speaking, word of wisdom is what Jesus would do in any given situation. Commonly used alongside the other revelatory gifts, words of wisdom are actual wisdom that God gives us to help us know how to apply our plans and even other prophetic words to our lives. When it is a word, wisdom is like instruction. Think of it as heaven coaching you on how to plan and pursue who you are or what you're called to, or how to love those who are your destiny.

DISCERNMENT

Discernment is God-inspired identification of an unseen spiritual reality. We receive it by hearing from God. All discernment is based off of perceiving from God the variables of good versus evil in any given person, place, thing or situation. We can apply discernment to every area of life. All of heaven can be discerned, as well as the things of this earth.

QUIZ EXAMPLES

With Contextual Understanding

1. Acts 9:12 (NASB): "and he has seen, in a vision a man named Ananias come in and lay his hands on him, so that he might regain his sight."

- WORD OF KNOWLEDGE
- PROPHECY
- DISCERNMENT
- WORD OF WISDOM

In Acts 9:12, a person saw a vision in the present tense. A divinely inspired fact about the person was shared. This is a word of knowledge.

---

2. Daniel 9:25 (NASB): "So you are to know and discern that from the issuing of a decree to restore and rebuild Jerusalem until Messiah the Prince there will be seven weeks and sixty-two weeks; it will be built again, with plaza and moat, even in times of distress."

- WORD OF KNOWLEDGE
- PROPHECY
- DISCERNMENT
- WORD OF WISDOM

This scripture forecasts a future event from the heart and mind of God. Dates are given and future context is provided. This is a prophecy.

---

3. John 4:19 (NASB): "The woman said to Him, 'Sir, I perceive that You are a prophet.'"

- WORD OF KNOWLEDGE
- PROPHECY
- DISCERNMENT
- WORD OF WISDOM

John 4:19 shows divine identification of the gift of God on someone's life. This is discernment.

4. Luke 19:30-31 (NASB): "Go into the village ahead of you; there, as you enter, you will find a colt tied on which no one yet has ever sat; untie it and bring it here. If anyone asks you, 'Why are you untying it?' you shall say, 'The Lord has need of it.'"

- WORD OF KNOWLEDGE
- PROPHECY
- DISCERNMENT
- WORD OF WISDOM

This verse illustrates God-given facts about the location and discovery of a colt, along with the conversation that is about to take place. Luke 19:30-31 took place in the present context. This would be considered a word of knowledge.

---

5. Matthew 22:15-22 (NASB): "Then the Pharisees went and plotted together how they might trap Him in what He said. And they sent their disciples to Him, along with the Herodians, saying, 'Teacher, we know that You are truthful and teach the way of God in truth, and defer to no one; for You are not partial to any. Tell us then, what do You think? Is it lawful to give a poll-tax to Caesar, or not?' But Jesus perceived their malice, and said, 'Why are you testing Me, you hypocrites? Show Me the coin used for the poll-tax.' And they brought Him a denarius. And He said to them, 'Whose likeness and inscription is this?' They said to Him, 'Caesar's.' Then He said to them, 'Then render to Caesar the things that are Caesar's; and to God the things that are God's.' And hearing this, they were amazed, and leaving Him, they went away."

- WORD OF KNOWLEDGE
- PROPHECY
- DISCERNMENT
- WORD OF WISDOM

In Matthew 22:15-22, we see a word of wisdom: In the midst of options, wisdom provided the best solution.

ANSWERS TO CHAPTER QUIZZES

CHAPTER ONE

1. Acts 9:12 (NASB)
and he has seen, in a vision a man named Ananias come in and lay his hands on him, so that he might regain his sight."

    a. WORD OF KNOWLEDGE   b. PROPHECY
    c. DISCERNMENT   d. WORD OF WISDOM

2. Daniel 9:25 (NASB)
So you are to know and discern that from the issuing of a decree to restore and rebuild Jerusalem until Messiah the Prince there will be seven weeks and sixty-two weeks; it will be built again, with plaza and moat, even in times of distress.

    a. WORD OF KNOWLEDGE   b. PROPHECY
    c. DISCERNMENT   c. WORD OF WISDOM

3. John 4:19 (NASB)
The woman said to Him, "Sir, I perceive that You are a prophet.

    a. WORD OF KNOWLEDGE   b. PROPHECY
    c. DISCERNMENT   d. WORD OF WISDOM

4. Luke 19:30-31 (NASB)
30 saying, "Go into the village ahead of you; there, as you enter, you will find a colt tied on which no one yet has ever sat; untie it and bring it here. 31 If anyone asks you, 'Why are you untying it?' you shall say, 'The Lord has need of it.'"

    a. WORD OF KNOWLEDGE   b. PROPHECY
    c. DISCERNMENT   d. WORD OF WISDOM

5. Matthew 22:15-22 (NASB)

¹⁵ Then the Pharisees went and plotted together how they might trap Him in what He said. ¹⁶ And they *sent their disciples to Him, along with the Herodians, saying, "Teacher, we know that You are truthful and teach the way of God in truth, and defer to no one; for You are not partial to any. ¹⁷ Tell us then, what do You think? Is it lawful to give a poll-tax to Caesar, or not?" ¹⁸ But Jesus perceived their malice, and said, "Why are you testing Me, you hypocrites? ¹⁹ Show Me the coin used for the poll-tax." And they brought Him a denarius. ²⁰ And He *said to them, "Whose likeness and inscription is this?" ²¹ They *said to Him, "Caesar's." Then He *said to them, "Then render to Caesar the things that are Caesar's; and to God the things that are God's." ²² And hearing this, they were amazed, and leaving Him, they went away.

a. WORD OF KNOWLEDGE   b. PROPHECY
c. DISCERNMENT   d. WORD OF WISDOM

CHAPTER TWO

1. Genesis 15:5 (NASB)

"And He took him outside and said, 'Now look toward the heavens, and count the stars, if you are able to count them.' And He said to him, 'So shall your descendants be.'"

a. WORD OF KNOWLEDGE   b. PROPHECY
c. DISCERNMENT   d. WORD OF WISDOM

2. 2 Kings 4:9 (NASB)

"She said to her husband, 'Behold now, I perceive that this is a holy man of God passing by us continually.'"

a. WORD OF KNOWLEDGE   b. PROPHECY
c. DISCERNMENT   c. WORD OF WISDOM

3. Mark 14:13-15 (NASB)

"And He sent two of His disciples and said to them, 'Go into the city, and a man will meet you carrying a pitcher of water; follow him; and wherever he enters, say to the owner of the house, "The Teacher says, 'Where is My guest room in which I may eat the Passover with My disciples?'" And he himself will show you a large upper room furnished and ready; prepare for us there.'"

a. WORD OF KNOWLEDGE   b. PROPHECY
c. DISCERNMENT   d. WORD OF WISDOM

4. Luke 4:1-14 (NASB)

"Jesus, full of the Holy Spirit, returned from the Jordan and was led around by the Spirit in the wilderness for forty days, being tempted by the devil. And He ate nothing during those days, and when they had ended, He became hungry. And the devil said to Him, 'If You are the Son of God, tell this stone to become bread.' And Jesus answered him, 'It is written, "Man shall not live on bread alone."' And he led Him up and showed Him all the kingdoms of the world in a moment of time. And the devil said to Him, 'I will give You all this domain and its glory; for it has been handed over to me, and I give it to whomever I wish. Therefore, if You worship before me, it shall all be Yours.' Jesus answered him, 'It is written, "You shall worship the Lord your God and serve Him only."' And he led Him to Jerusalem and had Him stand on the pinnacle of the temple, and said to Him, 'If You are the Son of God, throw Yourself down from here; for it is written, "He will command His angels concerning You to guard You," and, "On their hands they will bear You up, So that You will not strike Your foot against a stone."' And Jesus answered and said to him, 'It is said, "You shall not put the Lord your God to the test."' When the devil had finished every temptation, he left Him until an opportune time. And Jesus returned to Galilee in the power of the Spirit, and news about Him spread through all the surrounding district."

a. WORD OF KNOWLEDGE   b. PROPHECY
c. DISCERNMENT   **d. WORD OF WISDOM**

5. Matthew 16:16-18 (NASB)

"Simon Peter answered, 'You are the Christ, the Son of the living God.' And Jesus said to him, 'Blessed are you, Simon Barjona, because flesh and blood did not reveal this to you, but My Father who is in heaven. I also say to you that you are Peter, and upon this rock I will build My church; and the gates of Hades will not overpower it.'"

a. WORD OF KNOWLEDGE   **b. PROPHECY**
c. DISCERNMENT   d. WORD OF WISDOM

CHAPTER THREE

1. Genesis: 45:5-8 (NASB)

"Now do not be grieved or angry with yourselves, because you sold me here, for God sent me before you to preserve life. For the famine has been in the land these two years, and there are still five years in which there will be neither plowing nor harvesting. God sent me before you to preserve for you a remnant in the earth, and to keep you alive by a great deliverance. Now, therefore, it was not you who sent me here, but God; and He has made me a father to Pharaoh and lord of all his household and ruler over all the land of Egypt."

a. WORD OF KNOWLEDGE   b. PROPHECY
c. DISCERNMENT   **d. WORD OF WISDOM**

2. 2 Kings 6:8-12 (NIV)

"Now the king of Aram was at war with Israel. After conferring with his officers, he said, 'I will set up my camp in such and such a place.' The man of God sent word to the king of Israel: 'Beware of passing that place, because the Arameans are going down there.' So the king of Israel checked on the place indicated by the man of God. Time and again Elisha warned the king, so that he was on his guard in such places. This enraged the king of Aram. He summoned his officers and demanded of them, 'Tell me! Which of us is on the side of the king of Israel?' 'None of us, my lord the king,' said one of his officers, 'but Elisha, the prophet who is in Israel, tells the king of Israel the very words you speak in your bedroom.'"

<table>
<tr><td>a. WORD OF KNOWLEDGE</td><td>b. PROPHECY</td></tr>
<tr><td>c. DISCERNMENT</td><td>c. WORD OF WISDOM</td></tr>
</table>

3. Mark 2:8 (NIV)

"Immediately Jesus knew in his spirit that this was what they were thinking in their hearts, and he said to them, 'Why are you thinking these things?'"

<table>
<tr><td>a. WORD OF KNOWLEDGE</td><td>b. PROPHECY</td></tr>
<tr><td>c. DISCERNMENT</td><td>d. WORD OF WISDOM</td></tr>
</table>

4. Deuteronomy 18:15 (NIV)

"The Lord your God will raise up for you a prophet like me from among you, from your fellow Israelites. You must listen to him."

<table>
<tr><td>a. WORD OF KNOWLEDGE</td><td>b. PROPHECY</td></tr>
<tr><td>c. DISCERNMENT</td><td>d. WORD OF WISDOM</td></tr>
</table>

5. 1 Samuel 9:15-21 (NIV)

"Now the day before Saul came, the Lord had revealed this to Samuel: 'About this time tomorrow I will send you a man from the land of Benjamin. Anoint him ruler over my people Israel; he will deliver them from the hand of the Philistines. I have looked on my people, for their cry has reached me.' When Samuel caught sight of Saul, the Lord said to him, 'This is the man I spoke to you about; he will govern my people.' Saul approached Samuel in the gateway and asked, 'Would you please tell me where the seer's house is?' "'I am the seer,' Samuel replied. 'Go up ahead of me to the high place, for today you are to eat with me, and in the morning I will send you on your way and will tell you all that is in your heart. As for the donkeys you lost three days ago, do not worry about them; they have been found. And to whom is all the desire of Israel turned, if not to you and your whole family line?' "Saul answered, 'But am I not a Benjamite, from the smallest tribe of Israel, and is not my clan the least of all the clans of the tribe of Benjamin? Why do you say such a thing to me?'"

<table>
<tr><td>a. WORD OF KNOWLEDGE</td><td>b. PROPHECY</td></tr>
<tr><td>c. DISCERNMENT</td><td>d. WORD OF WISDOM</td></tr>
</table>

CHAPTER FOUR

1. Matthew 17:27 (NIV)
"But so that we may not cause offense, go to the lake and throw out your line. Take the first fish you catch; open its mouth and you will find a four-drachma coin. Take it and give it to them for my tax and yours."

a. WORD OF KNOWLEDGE   b. PROPHECY
c. DISCERNMENT   d. WORD OF WISDOM

2. John 2:19-22 (NIV)
"They replied, 'It has taken forty-six years to build this temple, and you are going to raise it in three days?' But the temple he had spoken of was his body. After he was raised from the dead, his disciples recalled what he had said. Then they believed the scripture and the words that Jesus had spoken."

a. WORD OF KNOWLEDGE   b. PROPHECY
c. DISCERNMENT   c. WORD OF WISDOM

3. Acts 21:10-11 (NASB)
"As we were staying there for some days, a prophet named Agabus came down from Judea. And coming to us, he took Paul's belt and bound his own feet and hands, and said, 'This is what the Holy Spirit says: "In this way the Jews at Jerusalem will bind the man who owns this belt and deliver him into the hands of the Gentiles."'"

a. WORD OF KNOWLEDGE   b. PROPHECY
c. DISCERNMENT   d. WORD OF WISDOM

4. Micah 5:2 (NIV)
"But you, Bethlehem Ephrathah, though you are small among the clans of Judah, out of you will come for me one who will be ruler over Israel, whose origins are from of old, from ancient times."

a. WORD OF KNOWLEDGE   b. PROPHECY
c. DISCERNMENT   d. WORD OF WISDOM

5. Acts 23:6 (NASB)
"But perceiving that one group were Sadducees and the other Pharisees, Paul began crying out in the Council, 'Brethren, I am a Pharisee, a son of Pharisees; I am on trial for the hope and resurrection of the dead!'"

a. WORD OF KNOWLEDGE   b. PROPHECY
c. DISCERNMENT   d. WORD OF WISDOM

CHAPTER FIVE

1. Acts 8:23 (NLT)
"... for I can see that you are full of bitter jealousy and are held captive by sin."

a. WORD OF KNOWLEDGE   b. PROPHECY
c. DISCERNMENT   d. WORD OF WISDOM

2. Genesis 41:1-37 (NASB)
"Now it happened at the end of two full years that Pharaoh had a dream, and behold, he was standing by the Nile. And lo, from the Nile there came up seven cows, sleek and fat; and they grazed in the marsh grass. Then behold, seven other cows came up after them from the Nile, ugly and gaunt, and they stood by the other cows on the bank of the Nile. The ugly and gaunt cows ate up the seven sleek and fat cows. Then Pharaoh awoke. He fell asleep and dreamed a second time; and behold, seven ears of grain came up on a single stalk, plump and good. Then behold, seven ears, thin and scorched by the east wind, sprouted up after them. The thin ears swallowed up the seven plump and full ears. Then Pharaoh awoke, and behold, it was a dream. Now in the morning his spirit was troubled, so he sent and called for all the magicians of Egypt, and all its wise men. And Pharaoh told them his dreams, but there was no one who could interpret them to Pharaoh. Then the chief cupbearer spoke to Pharaoh, saying, 'I would make mention today of my own offenses. Pharaoh was furious with his servants, and he put me in confinement in the house of the captain of the bodyguard, both me and the chief baker. We had a dream on the same night, he and I; each of us dreamed according to the interpretation of his own dream. Now a Hebrew youth was with us there, a servant of the captain of the bodyguard, and we related them to him, and he interpreted our dreams for us. To each one he interpreted according to his own dream. And just as he interpreted for us, so it happened; he restored me in my office, but he hanged him.' Then Pharaoh sent and called for Joseph, and they hurriedly brought him out of the dungeon; and when he had shaved himself and changed his clothes, he came to Pharaoh. Pharaoh said to Joseph, 'I have had a dream, but no one can interpret it; and I have heard it said about you, that when you hear a dream you can interpret it.' Joseph then answered Pharaoh, saying, 'It is not in me; God will give Pharaoh a favorable answer.' So Pharaoh spoke to Joseph, 'In my dream, behold, I was standing on the bank of the Nile; and behold, seven cows, fat and sleek came up out of the Nile, and they grazed in the marsh grass. Lo, seven other cows came up after them, poor and very ugly and gaunt, such as I had never seen for ugliness in all the land of Egypt; and the lean and ugly cows ate up the first seven fat cows. Yet when they had devoured them, it could not be detected that they had devoured them, for they were just as ugly as before. Then I awoke. I saw also in my dream, and behold, seven ears, full and good, came up on a single stalk; and lo, seven ears, withered, thin, and scorched by the east wind, sprouted up after them; and the thin ears swallowed the seven good ears. Then I told it to the magicians, but there was no one who could explain it to me.' Now Joseph said to Pharaoh, 'Pharaoh's dreams

are one and the same; God has told to Pharaoh what He is about to do. The seven good cows are seven years; and the seven good ears are seven years; the dreams are one and the same. The seven lean and ugly cows that came up after them are seven years, and the seven thin ears scorched by the east wind will be seven years of famine. It is as I have spoken to Pharaoh: God has shown to Pharaoh what He is about to do. Behold, seven years of great abundance are coming in all the land of Egypt; and after them seven years of famine will come, and all the abundance will be forgotten in the land of Egypt, and the famine will ravage the land. So the abundance will be unknown in the land because of that subsequent famine; for it will be very severe. Now as for the repeating of the dream to Pharaoh twice, it means that the matter is determined by God, and God will quickly bring it about. Now let Pharaoh look for a man discerning and wise, and set him over the land of Egypt. Let Pharaoh take action to appoint overseers in charge of the land, and let him exact a fifth of the produce of the land of Egypt in the seven years of abundance. Then let them gather all the food of these good years that are coming, and store up the grain for food in the cities under Pharaoh's authority, and let them guard it. Let the food become as a reserve for the land for the seven years of famine which will occur in the land of Egypt, so that the land will not perish during the famine.' Now the proposal seemed good to Pharaoh and to all his servants."

a. WORD OF KNOWLEDGE   b. PROPHECY
c. DISCERNMENT   c. WORD OF WISDOM

3. 1 King 19:15-16 (NIV)

"Then the Lord told him, 'Go back the same way you came, and travel to the wilderness of Damascus. When you arrive there, anoint Hazael to be king of Aram. Then anoint Jehu grandson of Nimshi to be king of Israel, and anoint Elisha son of Shaphat from the town of Abel-meholah to replace you as my prophet.'"

a. WORD OF KNOWLEDGE   b. PROPHECY
c. DISCERNMENT   d. WORD OF WISDOM

4. John 1:43-51 (NASB)

"The next day He purposed to go into Galilee, and He found Philip. And Jesus said to him, 'Follow Me.' Now Philip was from Bethsaida, of the city of Andrew and Peter. Philip found Nathanael and said to him, 'We have found Him of whom Moses in the Law and also the Prophets wrote—Jesus of Nazareth, the son of Joseph.' Nathanael said to him, 'Can any good thing come out of Nazareth?' Philip said to him, 'Come and see.' Jesus saw Nathanael coming to Him, and said of him, 'Behold, an Israelite indeed, in whom there is no deceit!' Nathanael said to Him, 'How do You know me?' Jesus answered and said to him, 'Before Philip called you, when you were under the fig tree, I saw you.' Nathanael answered Him, 'Rabbi, You are the Son of God; You are the King of Israel.' Jesus answered and said to him, 'Because I said to you that I saw you under the fig tree, do you believe? You will see greater things than these.' And He said to him, 'Truly, truly, I say to you, you will see the heavens opened and the angels of God ascending and descending on the Son of Man.'"

    a. WORD OF KNOWLEDGE   b. PROPHECY
    c. DISCERNMENT   d. WORD OF WISDOM

5. Isaiah 7:14 (NASB)
"Therefore the Lord Himself will give you a sign: Behold, a virgin will be with child and bear a son, and she will call His name Immanuel."

    a. WORD OF KNOWLEDGE   b. PROPHECY
    c. DISCERNMENT   d. WORD OF WISDOM

CHAPTER SIX

1. Acts 9:11-16 (NASB)
"And the Lord said to him, 'Get up and go to the street called Straight, and inquire at the house of Judas for a man from Tarsus named Saul, for he is praying, and he has seen in a vision a man named Ananias come in and lay his hands on him, so that he might regain his sight.' But Ananias answered, 'Lord, I have heard from many about this man, how much harm he did to Your saints at Jerusalem; and here he has authority from the chief priests to bind all who call on Your name.' But the Lord said to him, 'Go, for he is a chosen instrument of Mine, to bear My name before the Gentiles and kings and the sons of Israel; for I will show him how much he must suffer for My name's sake.'"

    a. WORD OF KNOWLEDGE   b. PROPHECY
    c. DISCERNMENT   d. WORD OF WISDOM

2. Matthew 22:18 (NASB)
"But Jesus perceived their malice, and said, 'Why are you testing Me, you hypocrites?'"

    a. WORD OF KNOWLEDGE   b. PROPHECY
    c. DISCERNMENT   c. WORD OF WISDOM

3. Acts 10:23-29 (NASB)
"So he invited them in and gave them lodging. And on the next day he got up and went away with them, and some of the brethren from Joppa accompanied him. On the following day he entered Caesarea. Now Cornelius was waiting for them and had called together his relatives and close friends. When Peter entered, Cornelius met him, and fell at his feet and worshiped him. But Peter raised him up, saying, 'Stand up; I too am just a man.' As he talked with him, he entered and found many people assembled. And he said to them, 'You yourselves know how unlawful it is for a man who is a Jew to associate with a foreigner or to visit him; and yet God has shown me that I should not call any man unholy or unclean. That is why I came without even rais-

ing any objection when I was sent for. So I ask for what reason you have sent for me.'"

a. WORD OF KNOWLEDGE   b. PROPHECY
c. DISCERNMENT   d. WORD OF WISDOM

4. Acts 16:9-11 (NIV)

"During the night Paul had a vision of a man of Macedonia standing and begging him, 'Come over to Macedonia and help us.' After Paul had seen the vision, we got ready at once to leave for Macedonia, concluding that God had called us to preach the gospel to them. From Troas we put out to sea and sailed straight for Samothrace, and the next day we went on to Neapolis."

a. WORD OF KNOWLEDGE   b. PROPHECY
c. DISCERNMENT   d. WORD OF WISDOM

5. Nehemiah 6:10-14 (NASB)

"When I entered the house of Shemaiah the son of Delaiah, son of Mehetabel, who was confined at home, he said, 'Let us meet together in the house of God, within the temple, and let us close the doors of the temple, for they are coming to kill you, and they are coming to kill you at night.' But I said, 'Should a man like me flee? And could one such as I go into the temple to save his life? I will not go in.' Then I perceived that surely God had not sent him, but he uttered his prophecy against me because Tobiah and Sanballat had hired him. He was hired for this reason, that I might become frightened and act accordingly and sin, so that they might have an evil report in order that they could reproach me. Remember, O my God, Tobiah and Sanballat according to these works of theirs, and also Noadiah the prophetess and the rest of the prophets who were trying to frighten me."

a. WORD OF KNOWLEDGE   b. PROPHECY
c. DISCERNMENT   d. WORD OF WISDOM

CHAPTER SEVEN

1. Isaiah 9:6-7 (NASB)

"For a child will be born to us, a son will be given to us; And the government will rest on His shoulders; And His name will be called Wonderful Counselor, Mighty God, Eternal Father, Prince of Peace. There will be no end to the increase of His government or of peace, On the throne of David and over his kingdom, to establish it and to uphold it with justice and righteousness from then on and forevermore. The zeal of the LORD of hosts will accomplish this."

a. WORD OF KNOWLEDGE   b. PROPHECY
c. DISCERNMENT   d. WORD OF WISDOM

2. Acts 10:22 (NASB)

"They said, 'Cornelius, a centurion, a righteous and God-fearing man well spoken of by the entire nation of the Jews, was divinely directed by a holy angel to send for you to come to his house and hear a message from you.'"

a. WORD OF KNOWLEDGE   b. PROPHECY
c. DISCERNMENT   c. WORD OF WISDOM

3. Acts 10:34 (NASB)

"Opening his mouth, Peter said, 'I most certainly understand now that God is not one to show partiality.'"

a. WORD OF KNOWLEDGE   b. PROPHECY
c. DISCERNMENT   d. WORD OF WISDOM

4. 1 Kings 19:14-18 (NASB)

"Then he said, 'I have been very zealous for the Lord, the God of hosts; for the sons of Israel have forsaken Your covenant, torn down Your altars and killed Your prophets with the sword. And I alone am left; and they seek my life, to take it away.' The Lord said to him, 'Go, return on your way to the wilderness of Damascus, and when you have arrived, you shall anoint Hazael king over Aram; and Jehu the son of Nimshi you shall anoint king over Israel; and Elisha the son of Shaphat of Abel-meholah you shall anoint as prophet in your place. It shall come about, the one who escapes from the sword of Hazael, Jehu shall put to death, and the one who escapes from the sword of Jehu, Elisha shall put to death. Yet I will leave 7,000 in Israel, all the knees that have not bowed to Baal and every mouth that has not kissed him.'"

a. WORD OF KNOWLEDGE   b. PROPHECY
c. DISCERNMENT   d. WORD OF WISDOM

5. Acts 15:19-22 (NASB)

"'Therefore, it is my judgment that we do not trouble those who are turning to God from among the Gentiles, but that we write to them that they abstain from things contaminated by idols and from fornication and from what is strangled and from blood. For Moses from ancient generations has in every city those who preach him, since he is read in the synagogues every Sabbath.' Then it seemed good to the apostles and the elders, with the whole church, to choose men from among them to send to Antioch with Paul and Barnabas—Judas called Barsabbas, and Silas, leading men among the brethren."

a. WORD OF KNOWLEDGE   b. PROPHECY
c. DISCERNMENT   d. WORD OF WISDOM

CHAPTER EIGHT

1. Acts 10:1-6 (ESV)

"At Caesarea there was a man named Cornelius, a centurion of what was known as the Italian Cohort, a devout man who feared God with all his household, gave alms generously to the people, and prayed continually to God. About the ninth hour of the day, he saw clearly in a vision an angel of God come in and say to him, 'Cornelius.' And he stared at him in terror and said, 'What is it, Lord?' And he said to him, 'Your prayers and your alms have ascended as a memorial before God. And now send men to Joppa and bring one Simon who is called Peter. He is lodging with one Simon, a tanner, whose house is by the sea.'"

a. WORD OF KNOWLEDGE   b. PROPHECY
c. DISCERNMENT   d. WORD OF WISDOM

2. Acts 6:2-6 (NASB)

"So the twelve summoned the congregation of the disciples and said, 'It is not desirable for us to neglect the word of God in order to serve tables. Therefore, brethren, select from among you seven men of good reputation, full of the Spirit and of wisdom, whom we may put in charge of this task. But we will devote ourselves to prayer and to the ministry of the word.' The statement found approval with the whole congregation; and they chose Stephen, a man full of faith and of the Holy Spirit, and Philip, Prochorus, Nicanor, Timon, Parmenas and Nicolas, a proselyte from Antioch. And these they brought before the apostles; and after praying, they laid their hands on them."

a. WORD OF KNOWLEDGE   b. PROPHECY
c. DISCERNMENT   c. WORD OF WISDOM

3. Luke 1:11-12 (NASB)

"And an angel of the Lord appeared to him, standing to the right of the altar of incense. Zacharias was troubled when he saw the angel, and fear gripped him."

a. WORD OF KNOWLEDGE   b. PROPHECY
c. DISCERNMENT   d. WORD OF WISDOM

4. Genesis 37:5-11 (NIV)

"Joseph had a dream, and when he told it to his brothers, they hated him all the more. He said to them, 'Listen to this dream I had: We were binding sheaves of grain out in the field when suddenly my sheaf rose and stood upright, while your sheaves gathered around mine and bowed down to it.' His brothers said to him, 'Do you intend to reign over us? Will you actually rule us?' And they hated him all the more because of his dream and what he had said. Then he had another dream, and he told it to his brothers. 'Listen,' he said, 'I had another dream, and this time the sun and moon and eleven stars were bowing down to me.' When he told his father as well as his brothers, his father rebuked him and said, 'What is this dream you had? Will your mother and I and your brothers actually come and bow down to the ground before you?' His brothers were jealous of him, but his father kept the matter in mind."

a. WORD OF KNOWLEDGE   b. PROPHECY
c. DISCERNMENT   d. WORD OF WISDOM

5. John 4:4-26 (NASB)

"And He had to pass through Samaria. So He came to a city of Samaria called Sychar, near the parcel of ground that Jacob gave to his son Joseph; and Jacob's well was there. So Jesus, being wearied from His journey, was sitting thus by the well. It was about the sixth hour. There came a woman of Samaria to draw water. Jesus said to her, 'Give Me a drink.' For His disciples had gone away into the city to buy food. Therefore the Samaritan woman said to Him, 'How is it that You, being a Jew, ask me for a drink since I am a Samaritan woman?' (For Jews have no dealings with Samaritans.) Jesus answered and said to her, 'If you knew the gift of God, and who it is who says to you, "Give Me a drink," you would have asked Him, and He would have given you living water.' She said to Him, 'Sir, You have nothing to draw with and the well is deep; where then do You get that living water? You are not greater than our father Jacob, are You, who gave us the well, and drank of it himself and his sons and his cattle?' Jesus answered and said to her, 'Everyone who drinks of this water that I will give him shall never thirst; but the water that I will give him will become in him a well of water springing up to eternal life.' The woman said to Him, 'Sir, give me this water, so I will not be thirsty nor come all the way here to draw.' He said to her, 'Go, call your husband and come here.' The woman answered and said, 'I have no husband.' Jesus said to her, 'You have correctly said, "I have no husband"; for you have had five husbands, and the one whom you now have is not your husband; this you have said truly.' The woman said to Him, 'Sir, I perceive that You are a prophet. Our fathers worshiped in this mountain, and you people say that in Jerusalem is the place where men ought to worship.' Jesus said to her, 'Woman, believe Me, an hour is coming when neither in this mountain nor in Jerusalem will you worship the Father. You worship what you do not know; we worship what we know, for salvation is from the Jews. But an hour is coming, and now is, when the true worshipers will worship the Father in spirit and truth; for such people the Father seeks to be His worshipers. God is spirit, and those who worship Him must worship in spirit and truth.' The woman said to Him, 'I know that Messiah is coming (He who is called Christ); when that One comes, He will declare all things to us.' Jesus said to her, 'I who speak to you am He.'"

a. WORD OF KNOWLEDGE   b. PROPHECY
c. DISCERNMENT   d. WORD OF WISDOM

QUIZ KEY

CHAPTER 1

1. Word of Knowledge
2. Prophecy
3. Discernment
4. Word of Knowledge
5. Word of Wisdom

CHAPTER 2

1. Prophecy
2. Discernment
3. Word of Knowledge
4. Word of Wisdom
5. Prophecy

CHAPTER 3

1. Word of Wisdom
2. Word of Knowledge
3. Discernment
4. Prophecy
5. Word of Knowledge

CHAPTER 4

1. Word of Knowledge
2. Prophecy
3. Word of Wisdom
4. Prophecy
5. Discernment

CHAPTER 5

1. Discernment
2. Word of Wisdom
3. Word of Knowledge
4. Word of Knowledge
5. Prophecy

CHAPTER 6

1. Word of Knowledge
2. Discernment
3. Word of Wisdom
4. Word of Knowledge
5. Discernment

CHAPTER 7

1. Prophecy
2. Word of Knowledge
3. Discernment
4. Word of Knowledge
5. Word of Wisdom

CHAPTER 8

1. Word of Knowledge
2. Word of Wisdom
3. Discernment
4. Prophecy
5. Word of Knowledge

ABOUT THE AUTHOR

Shawn is an international speaker, TV host, spiritual adviser, producer, minister, and best-selling author of Translating God, among others. Well known for his strong prophetic gift and fresh biblical perspective, Shawn is passionate about seeing God's love, creativity, and justice ministered through God's people today. Shawn is also the founding pastor of Expression58 Church, a mission base and church focused on training and equipping Christians, encouraging the creative arts, and loving people in the entertainment industry and those in need. He lives in Los Angeles, California, with his lovely wife, Cherie, and wonderful daughters, Harper and Hartley.

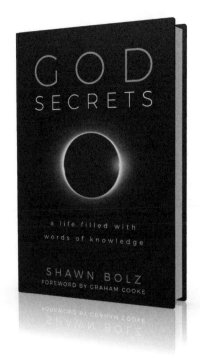

GOD SECRETS

a life filled with words of knowledge

YOU CAN KNOW THE SECRETS OF GOD

AND USE THAT KNOWLEDGE TO TRANSFORM THE WORLD AROUND YOU!

Shawn Bolz shares his stories, thoughts, and biblical understanding to give you the keys to access the secrets of God.

People are paying millions of dollars for information and understanding on matters like business, economics, and politics. God has the answers, and He has made His secrets discoverable to every seeking believer in a close relationship with Him. In *GOD SECRETS*, you'll learn how to:

- Gain access to God's deep knowledge and wisdom
- Share God's mindset
- Inspire and empower others with God's thoughts and dreams
- Use words of knowledge in everyday life scenarios
- Connect with His love for all of His creation, which includes you

God's secrets are shared through words of knowledge, one of His most misunderstood revelatory gifts. Journey with Shawn as he lays out this gift in a relatable way, and gain a fresh perspective on God's direction for your business, your household, and your worldview.

GOD WANTS YOU TO DISCOVER HIS SECRETS. IT WILL CHANGE YOU AND THE WORLD AROUND YOU.

GOD
SECRETS
a life filled with
words of knowledge

e-COURSE

GOD WANTS TO GIVE YOU FULL ACCESS TO HIS SECRETS

Shawn Bolz has shared his book God Secrets with you. Now take his eCourse, designed to activate the gift of words of knowledge in your own life and release its power.

Join Shawn as he takes you through 5+ hours of teaching and activations to help bring you into a deeper understanding of words of knowledge and their application today. Either individually or in a group, grow in the following areas:

SESSION 1: **Foundation**
Learn the history and benefits giving words of knowledge.

SESSION 2: **Intimacy**
Desire to know God's heart above all else.

SESSION 3: **Identity**
Be real, be you.

SESSION 4: **Accountability**
Grow in wisdom and humility with people you can trust.

SESSION 5: **Risk**
Be brave, heal from fear or the need to perform.

SESSION 6: **Hearing Ability**
So many ways to hear His voice; you cannot fail.

SESSION 7: **Delivery**
Share from a heart of love in a relevant way.

SESSION 8: **Faith**
There's always room for more.

Get this biblically based eCourse to get the most out of Shawn Bolz's book God Secrets: A Life Filled with Words of Knowledge, and watch this gift fulfill your own life and that of everyone around you.

TRANSLATING GOD

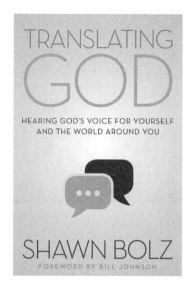

Through a thought-provoking prophetic ministry philosophy and Shawn's glorious successes and very real failures, you will be inspired and equipped to: learn how to hear God for yourself and others, grow through simple focused steps, take great risks, stay accountable, love people well, grow in intimacy with the Lord.

As an internationally known prophetic voice who has ministered to thousands from royalty to those on the streets Shawn shares everything he has learned about the prophetic in a way that is totally unique and refreshing. Shawn aims for the higher goal of loving people relationally, not just pursuing the gift or information, and he activates you to do the same.

Start to reshape the world around you with God's love today.

TRANSLATING GOD WORKBOOK

Be activated by Shawn's inspirational stories and use the activations, questions, and forms he includes in this life-altering workbook to chart your progress. Either individually or in a group, learn how to:

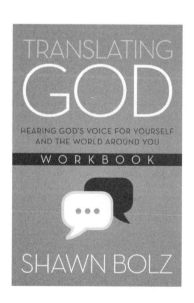

- Develop your relationship with God and others.
- Receive and understand revelation.
- Intentionally develop and nurture your prophetic ability.
- Become the fullness of God's expression of love through his revelation and voice.

TRANSLATING GOD
STUDY COURSE

GOD IS SPEAKING EVERY DAY, AND YOU CAN BE HIS MOUTHPIECE.

Sometimes figuring out how to do that can feel overwhelming, but the prophetic can become a completely natural and love-filled part of your life.

You have the chance to help reveal the nature of God and show his heart of love through your prophetic gift. Hearing and sharing his voice is one of the most dynamic and exciting parts of Christianity, and it's actually one of the easiest gifts to pursue.

In this *Translating God* Study Course, Shawn gives you the practical tools you need to further develop your unique strengths and prophetic style. He also shares his insights, personal stories, and profound teaching perspectives to help you:

- Hear God clearly
- Apply God's love-filled revelation to your daily life and relationships
- Increase the depth and effectiveness of your prophetic gift

Translating God will change your perspective of the prophetic and bring depth to your revelation and prophetic voice. Shawn aims for the higher goal of loving people relationally, not just pursuing the gift or information, and he activates you through dynamic exercises that will help you practice doing the same. Great for individuals and group study!

This set includes:
- º 9 video sessions on 3 DVDs (35-55 minutes each)
- º *Translating God*: Paperback book
- º *Translating God*: Workbook
- º Poster: to advertise group studies

GROWING UP WITH GOD

Chapter Book

JOIN LUCAS AND MARIA AND FRIENDS ON THEIR EVERYDAY ADVENTURES IN FRIENDSHIP WITH GOD!

Lucas knows God talks to him, but he would have never imagined that he would hear such a specific thing about his year . . . and could Maria really have heard God about her destiny? They both have to wonder if God speaks to kids this way. Over the months that follow, God begins to connect them to other kids that grow into friends. Who could have guessed that by the end of the year, their lives would be so exciting!

Award-winning illustrator Lamont Hunt illustrates the rich, vibrant God journey of kids you can relate to. By best-selling author Shawn Bolz.

Workbook

An accompaniment for *Growing Up with God*, the children's chapter book, this workbook will encourage your kids to practice hearing God's voice.

Not only does this workbook teach children how to listen to God, it also gives them the tools they need to support and believe in themselves and each other.

In each section that relates to a chapter in *Growing Up with God*, your children will find:

- A reminder of what was in the chapter
- A true story from a kid their age about how he or she encountered God
- Three important things to know about God's voice
- Bible verses to back up the teaching
- Questions for them to think about and answer
- A prayer
- Illustrations from the book to keep the content focused & exciting

This generation of kids will be the most powerful, prophetic generation yet, and this workbook is a journal and guide will help them fulfill that destiny.

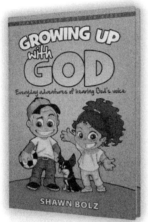